Jack Bauer for President

TERRORISM AND POLITICS IN 24

VISUAL & PERFORMING ARTS

EDITED BY

Richard Miniter

WITH LEAH WILSON

BENBELLA

BENBELLA BOOKS, INC.
Dallas, Texas

"Living with Terror" © 2008 by Jeanne Cavelos
"Can a Leftist Love 24?" © 2008 by Steven Rubio
"I Despise You for Making Me Do This" © 2008 by Brett Chandler Patterson
"Honey Traps, Romeos, and Blackmail" © 2008 by Paul Lytle
"Hacking Jack Bauer" © 2008 by Jim Rapoza
"Jack Bauer Is the Dirty Harry for the Age of Terrorism" © 2008 by Lorie Byrd
"Simulating Terror" © 2008 by Aaron Thomas Nelson
"The Third Degree" © 2008 by Christopher J. Patrick and Deborah L. Patrick
"24 and the Use of Torture to Obtain Preventive Intelligence" © 2008 by Alan M. Dershowitz
"The Reality of Interrogation" © 2008 by Eli Lake
"Jack (Bauer) and the Beanstalk" © 2008 by Daveed Gartenstein-Ross and Kyle Dabruzzi
"Hail to the Chief" © 2008 by Kristine Kathryn Rusch
"Jack Bauer Syndrome" © 2008 by Eric Greene

BenBella Books, Inc.
6440 N. Central Expressway, Suite 503
Dallas, TX 75206
www.benbellabooks.com
Send feedback to feedback@benbellabooks.com

Printed in the United States of America
10 9 8 7 6 5 4 3 2 1

Library of Congress Cataloging-in-Publication Data

Jack Bauer for president : terrorism and politics in 24 / edited by Richard Miniter, with Leah Wilson.
    p. cm.
  ISBN 1-933771-27-5
  1. 24 (Television program) 2. Terrorism on television. I. Miniter, Richard. II. Wilson, Leah.

  PN1992.77.A215J33 2007
  791.45'72--dc22
                        2007040263

Proofreading by Emily Chauvier and Stacia Seaman
Cover design by Todd Michael Bushman
Text design and composition by Laura Watkins
Printed by Bang Printing

Distributed by Independent Publishers Group
To order call (800) 888-4741
www.ipgbook.com

For special sales contact Robyn White at robyn@benbellabooks.com

Contents

Living with Terror

Jack Bauer as a Coping Mechanism in Post-Traumatic Stress Disordered America

JEANNE CAVELOS

When I was ten, my parents began leaving me home alone without a babysitter. They'd go to a dinner-dance, and I would sit on the floor of the faux-wood-paneled rec room in the cathode ray tube's glow, watching *The Six Million Dollar Man* or *The Brady Bunch*. The curtains would be closed against the night, yet again and again my attention would drift there, searching past the TV's flickering light on the fabric, certain that on the other side of the glass lurked a homicidal maniac.

As I spent more time alone, I developed a routine to help me cope with my fears. Horror movies had taught me a lot about facing homicidal maniacs. Make sure all the doors are locked; a carelessly half-shut door is an invitation to Michael Myers. Make sure that tiny gap between one curtain and the other is closed; Jason Voorhees loves peeking in those tiny cracks. If the howling wind and creaking walls are too threatening, get the poker. Having a weapon at the ready is always a good idea—though you have to make sure not to use it hastily and kill the policeman who has come to save you. No matter what you hear, never ever pull the curtain back to look, because that's when the Wolfman will be pressing his hairy face right up to the glass.

Horror movies gave my vague fears specific form, but they also helped me overcome my fears. They showed me that I could face the chainsaws, the hatchets, the butcher knives, the nightmares, and that I could survive. They gave me confidence. They gave me hope.

For others, confidence and hope in the face of fear comes from other sources. An entire generation, confronted by the possibility of an all-out attack by the U.S.S.R., was taught to "duck and cover"—the surefire technique to survive a nuclear blast. Simply dive beneath that schoolroom desk, cover your head with your hands, and everything will be all right. It might not be practical (I'd still want my poker to defend against the inevitable atomic mutants to follow), but it allowed us to cope. It gave us the illusion of some sort of control over our lives, in a world that was increasingly beyond anyone's control.

I grew up in the post-duck-and-cover world. My generation knew we wouldn't survive that all-out Soviet attack, but we weren't nearly as bothered by it as the previous generation. Fear of nuclear attack lurked in the background of our lives, seldom rearing its mushroom-cloud head.

In college I participated in a psychology experiment. For about two hours, I was asked about my fears of a nuclear attack. Did I think the U.S.S.R. would ever attack us? If there was a nuclear attack, did I think I would receive advance warning? Did I expect I would die instantly as the first bombs fell? How long did I think I could survive?

I don't know the purpose of the experiment, and I was never told the results, but after those two hours, I couldn't get the thought of a nuclear attack from my mind. I realized that it could happen at any moment, perhaps with no warning at all, and that if I didn't die instantly, I could suffer an agonizingly slow death from radiation and starvation. I didn't sleep at all that night, staring up at the ceiling, tracing missiles shooting through the night sky, waiting for the thump of detonation, the skin-melting blast. The extermination of mankind. Would it come this moment? Or this?

I realized that, up until that afternoon, I had lived with the danger of nuclear attack the same way I lived with my own breathing. As psychologists would say, I had become habituated to it. The danger had existed all of my life, and I'd become used to it. Since the bombs were an ocean and a continent away, and mentioned in the news mainly when treaties were reached regarding their reduction, this wasn't too hard. Just as we step into the shower each morning without fearing we will slip and die, we go about our daily lives without considering that nuclear annihilation might be one button-push away.

The psychology experiment brought the danger to the forefront of my mind, forcing me to experience it anew and providing no comforting guidelines as to how I might successfully survive. For about a month, I was haunted by the fear of imminent nuclear attack. Then, finally, the fear faded.

A NEW FEAR IS BORN

On September 11, we all gained a new and immediate fear. This one can't be battled with a locked door and a poker, or the illusory shelter of a school desk, and the danger is evolving so quickly that it's been impossible thus far to become habituated to it.

After the attacks, some people couldn't cope. Across America, therapists saw "an increase in anxiety disorders and depression" (Glazer). They found that "[i]t was no longer just combat soldiers and victims of crime, rape, and abuse who were experiencing psychological trauma, but thousands if not millions of Americans" (Arehart-Treichel 21). Anxiety over what might happen at any moment overwhelmed many of us. Even now, long after September 11, researchers are finding that "Americans are suffering lingering symptoms of anxiety and trauma" (Glazer). The effect on us has been profound—far stronger and longer lasting than those arising from other types of mass disasters: "Different types of disasters are thought to elicit different responses from affected populations. . . . Willful acts of terrorism are thought to evoke the most severe reactions" ("Epidemiology").

Why is terrorism more traumatizing than other disasters? In the case of many traumatic events, those affected have some degree of warning, some understanding that they are taking on a risk. One might buy a home in an area prone to floods or hurricanes, hear a fire alarm and choose not to evacuate, or enlist in the army. Psychologists believe that "events perceived as uncontrollable are more distressing than those perceived as controllable" (Giarratano 258). In fact, traumatized patients who blame themselves for the traumatic event recover more quickly than patients who feel the event was totally beyond their control.

Terrorist acts, designed to maximize the terror they evoke, usually occur without warning, to people who have not taken any particular risk beyond going to work or getting on a plane. This may partly explain why some people are so drawn to the idea of blaming the U.S. for the actions of terrorists; it may help them better cope with their fear to believe we were responsible. Other factors that affect the severity of the impact are the degree of terror felt, whether there were horrific images associated with the event, the amount of grief experienced, the suddenness, duration, and intensity of the trauma, and the damage and casualties suffered. Disasters in which several of these components are extreme carry "the highest risk for severe psychiatric impact" ("Epidemiology"). The planes flying into the towers, the people leaping to their deaths, the scattered wreckage of United 93, the collapse of the World Trade Center in a cloud of dust—for many of us, these images comprise the most frightening and horrifying event we have ever witnessed, striking so suddenly, intensely, and irrevocably that its effect continues to linger. While most of us did not lose loved ones on September 11, we did lose our belief in the safety of our country.

Psychologist Roberta Caplan writes, "For everyone there was a sense that safety in the world had been shaken" (qtd. in Glazer). Americans realized "that bad things can now happen to them, that invulnerability is an illusion" (Janoff-Bulman qtd. in Kellermann). When the president put the country on Orange Alert in 2003, "That notice set off a stampede to stores for basic security provisions such as flashlights and duct tape to help prepare for a chemical attack. It also set off a rush to specialty companies stocking such unlikely products as anti-radiation tablets and full-body protective suits" (Green C1). ApprovedGasMasks.com has been doing bumper-crop business. Their best-selling products include "the MSA Advantage 3200 mask ($195.95), replete with voice-emitter diaphragm and anti-anthrax filters, and Special Forces-brand nuclear, biological, and chemical suits ($47.50), olive-drab green" (Green C1). Perry Hitt, president of the company, says, "In the minds of some customers, their children's lives are on the line" (qtd. in Green C1). A radiation alarm disguised as a key chain is featured in ads touting the danger of a suitcase nuke.

You might think that we would have become habituated to the fear of a terrorist attack by now. Yet it is difficult for a threat to fade into the background of our lives when we are constantly reminded of it. Terrorist

4

attacks occur frequently, and in a post 9/11 world, they resonate power-fully in our minds, reawakening our fears, extending the duration of our trauma, making us feel that our "destiny is shaped by external forces by which [we] have no control" (Kellermann). It's not necessary that the attacks occur in our city or even in our country. Just as the psychology experiment I underwent in college forced me to experience my fears of nuclear annihilation anew, simply watching a news report about a sub-way bomb attack can stimulate our fears of terrorism. Further, terrorist threats are not static, as the danger from Soviet ICBMs was. The evolv-ing danger of new terrorist groups and new techniques prevents our habituation. It would be difficult to become habituated to the danger of slipping in the shower, too, if you woke each morning to find your shower redesigned in a new shape and coated with new, more slippery substances. Unable to habituate to the fear of terrorism, many repress it, a psychological trait called avoidance. Some go as far as denying that the danger exists. Most of us, however, are only too aware that the danger is all around us. It can take countless forms, attack in countless ways.

We hear warnings about threats posted on radical Islamic Web sites — another attack on a major city is coming, a super computer virus is com-ing. Attacks on local malls, attacks on schools. Attacks by plane, attacks by train, attacks by subway. Planes flown into nuclear power plants. Trucks with biological agents. Radiological bombs whose fallout could cover Manhattan. Suitcase nukes. Bombs in shoes. Bombs in shampoo bottles. Plastic guns. Box cutters, cuticle scissors. Smallpox. Anthrax. Poisoned water supplies. We hear of increased terrorist chatter. New training camps. Terrorists planning to sneak in through Mexico. Sleeper cells. Female bombers. Children hacking the heads off of Westerners and cheering at their success.

Today, a casual flip through the news channels reveals the headline, "Zawahiri calls for more Americans to be killed" (Studio B). There is no escaping these fears. As Bill Keller writes in the *New York Times*, what "Sept. 11 did was . . . give our nightmares legs" (22).

TERRORISM AND POST-TRAUMATIC STRESS DISORDER

The evolving nature of this threat increases our feelings of "fear, helpless-ness or horror" (Glazer). These feelings are key to the development of

Post-Traumatic Stress Disorder, and in fact, psychologists have discovered that exposure to detailed media coverage of terrorist attacks creates "symptoms similar to those of Post-Traumatic Stress Disorder" (Keinan, Sadeh, and Rosen 149). We have become a country of the traumatized.

Any one of the hundreds of terrorist plots we hear about could provide nightmares for a lifetime. How can we begin to cope, gain some measure of confidence, some sense of control, some hope? Psychologists believe that Post-Traumatic Stress Disorder, or PTSD, "occurs because of an individual's inability to intellectually and emotionally process a distressing experience" (Giarratano 110–111). Instead of processing the fearful situation, PTSD sufferers tend to repress their thoughts about it or avoid acknowledging it entirely. To help this processing occur and reach a positive resolution, psychologists use cognitive behavioral therapy, one of the most successful treatments of PTSD.

Three key elements of cognitive behavioral therapy—exposure, role-play, and cognitive restructuring—are exactly those provided by Jack Bauer and company on Monday night. In each episode, 24 provides its viewers with a three-step PTSD treatment program.

EXPOSURE AND THE JACK BAUER SCHOOL OF THERAPY

Psychologists rely on exposure to "facilitat[e] emotional processing," or in other words, to help PTSD patients face their fears (Giarratano 111). According to the International Society for Traumatic Stress Studies, exposure therapy is critical for dealing with PTSD: "no other treatment modality has such strong evidence for its efficacy" (qtd. in Glazer). In exposure therapy, psychologists try to keep their patients in a relaxed state while gradually exposing them to fear-related stimuli. They may ask the patient to imagine the fearful situation, to visit a place associated with the fear, to listen repeatedly to an audio tape of themselves describing the situation, or to experience the fear through computer-generated imagery.

Watching 24 serves much the same purpose. The show may not expose us to our fears as gradually and gently as a psychologist does, but like a bullet to the leg of a stubborn captive, it gets the job done. In fact, while many psychologists advocate graded or gradual exposure, some find flooding—sudden total exposure—effective (Giarratano 175). This is more in line with the Jack Bauer school of therapy.

Critical to the success of exposure therapy is "careful, repeated, detailed imagining of the trauma" (U.S. Department of Veterans Affairs). For the exposure to work, the fear must be given specific shape and form. It is not enough to imagine the vague possibility of a nuclear attack by terrorists. We must face it in all its detail and horror. Is there any place better to do this than on 24? Psychologists have found that processing our fear "not only requires the creation of an organized, unfragmented narrative, but also a more articulated one" (Amir, Stafford, et al qtd. in Giarratano 206). Fiction can provide this much better than the news, where the details of terrorists' actions are often unknown. We must see the danger develop and we must see it come to fruition. We must see the worst happen. No last-minute, James Bond, red-wire clipping to stop the timer with one second to doomsday. That may have worked during the Cold War. But we no longer have faith that disaster can be averted. While 24 occasionally allows its characters to dodge a bullet, the quality that truly distinguishes the show, and makes it so effective as a coping mechanism, is that all too often the bullet cannot be dodged. Our nightmares are realized. Doomsday arrives. And people die.

As we face this fear, we must remain in a relaxed state. While the psychology experiment I participated in exposed me to a fear, it did so while I was in an increasingly tense state, causing my fears to worsen. Similarly, the news may make us tense and afraid. But 24 is entertainment. We watch the program for enjoyment. For most of us, sitting on the couch in front of a good TV show is one of the most relaxing acts in our lives. In this relaxed state, we are able to face our fears without experiencing a strong fear-response to them. This allows us to inoculate ourselves against our fears, exposing ourselves to a small sample in a safe way so we are better able to cope with a larger, more dangerous outbreak. According to critic Edmund Wilson, we can "inoculate ourselves against panic at the real horrors loose on the earth . . . by injections of imaginary horror" (288). When we experience the fear in a relaxed state, the fearful situation becomes more manageable. We begin to believe (rightly or wrongly) that it will not bring the end of the world. We begin to feel more control over ourselves and our fear. Our anxiety diminishes.

On Day 6, 24 exposed us to one of our greatest fears: the possibility of nuclear attack by terrorists. Even more frightening, the weapon involved was a suitcase nuke. It's difficult to feel safe and secure as you go about your daily life when an object that is "24 by 16 by 8 inches fitted with three coffee can-size aluminum canisters filled with plutonium or uranium" can destroy you and everyone you know (Badkhen A8). Since 2001, the media has released numerous reports of suitcase nukes, first revealing that "Russia is believed to have developed extremely small nuclear weapons—'suitcase' bombs—probably with yields equivalent to 1,000 tons of TNT" (Broad, Engelberg, and Glanz A1), then following up by asserting that "84 of the devices cannot be accounted for" (Webster and Watson A1). If this isn't enough to get you hanging up your plastic sheeting, Ayman al-Zawahri, al-Qaeda's number two man, has bragged that "If you have $30 million, go to the black market in central Asia, contact any disgruntled Soviet scientist . . . dozens of smart briefcase bombs are available" (Badkhen A8).

Do the terrorists have suitcase nukes? Are they here? Are they ready? We need to face this fear if we are to cope with it. Here comes Jack Bauer to the rescue.

At the beginning of Day 6, Jack learns that the terrorist Fayed has smuggled a Russian suitcase nuke into the country. For the first time, our fear takes concrete form. As Fayed works to execute his plan, the shadowy device that has haunted our nightmares, "The Sum of All Fears" (in Tom Clancy's words), is finally brought into the light. From the outside, it looks perfectly harmless: a metal suitcase. Yet, as we contemplate it, and as we see Jack's desperate determination to find it, the truth of it sinks into our souls: inside that small package, which can be taken to any town or city in the country, lurk the horrors of Hiroshima and Nagasaki.

We see the fearful situation develop. Fayed needs a new component to detonate the bomb, and the trigger needs to be reprogrammed. He demands the government release a group of enemy combatants, one of whom is Numair, a nuclear engineer. Unable to stop the release, Jack struggles to track down Fayed and Numair. He learns that the nuke, referred to by the terrorists as "the visitor," arrived in the U.S. the week before, and that Numair is the key to making it operational. Fayed acquires the component, and Numair goes to work. The suitcase nuke is nearly ready to detonate.

For the exposure to be complete, we need to see the fear come to fruition. Jack discovers the location of Fayed's safe house, and CTU sends agents who move in. Under fire, Numair decides he has no choice. He detonates the suitcase nuke. Terrorists, CTU agents, civilians—all are enveloped in a blinding white flash, a sheet of sun that cuts through skin, bone, metal. The shock wave boils out, vaporizing bodies, ripping through walls, flattening buildings, hurtling outward, melting, inciner- ating, disintegrating, carrying its radioactive fallout into the air. Across the city, the brilliant flash slices across the sky. Jack looks upward. On his face we see the full horror of what has happened, and we feel that full horror. This is no longer a repressed, unprocessed fear; it is a vivid, intensely emotional experience. Our fear is finally realized. A mushroom cloud rises over Los Angeles. And CTU learns that the terrorists have four more bombs.

Exposure begins the coping process. We face our fear while maintain- ing our relaxed state. We start to become habituated to these terrorist scenarios, and we begin to feel some sort of control over ourselves and our emotions. After all, if we can enjoy terrorist plots as part of a TV show, we can "soothe [ourselves] with the momentary illusion that the forces of madness and murder may be tamed and compelled to provide us with a mere dramatic entertainment" (Wilson 288).

But to truly help us, the process must take us beyond facing dooms- day. We must consider how we might survive doomsday. If we fear black cats, then facing a few friendly black cats may be enough to conquer our fear. The black cat, after all, meant no harm in the first place. If we suf- fer from PTSD over a one-time event in our past, such as surviving a fire, then facing our fear can be enough: "The whole point of the treatment is to explain that a memory can't hurt you" (Yehuda qtd. in Glazer). But if we fear terrorism, exposure to the fear and habituation will only take us so far. Terrorists can still hurt us. Randall Marshall, director of Trauma Studies at the New York State Psychiatric Institute, describes the problem: "You can no longer say to a patient, 'That will never happen again'" (qtd. in Glazer).

ROLE-PLAY WITH CHLOE AND MORRIS

When we hear about new threats of a suitcase nuke about to be detonat- ed on American soil, we want not only control over ourselves and our fear, but the illusion, at least, of control over the situation. We must rehearse, or in psychological terms, role-play. While exposure helps us face our fear, role-playing allows us to explore the fearful situation from different perspectives and gain a greater understanding of it and our reactions to it. PTSD patients often re-enact the traumatic event in their lives, playing various roles in a process called psychodrama: "Based on the time-honored therapeutic principles of re-enactment and catharsis, as well as on the novel elements of ritual and narrative, psychodrama has been successfully employed with numerous traumatised clients for over fifty years" (Kellermann). Role-play allows us to work through our fearful experiences, engaging both our emotions and our thoughts and allowing us to further process them.

As we watch 24, we relate to the various characters, imagining what it would be like to be them, imagining what we would do in their situations. What is it like to be Morris O'Brian, captured by terrorists and threatened with death if we don't make their nuclear weapon operational? We suffer with Morris as they jam a squealing drill into his shoulder. We root for him to continue his defiance, yet we fear for his life. We imagine various alternatives he might try: jumping out a window, fighting, pretending to cooperate and sabotaging the bomb. We think about what we might do. In essence, we role-play.

Role-play works best when the PTSD sufferer is in a simultaneous state of "detachment and involvement" that allows him to re-experience fearful situations without becoming overwhelmed (Kellermann). Watching 24, we are detached, since the events aren't really happening to us, and yet involved, because we relate to the characters and care about them. So 24 provides the proper state for role-play to have its greatest effectiveness.

Role-play often includes the rehearsal of various possible behaviors. A rape victim might be asked to rehearse how she will behave the next time someone is walking behind her on a lonely street. Similarly, during 24, we vicariously enact behaviors we might use in the fearful situation. We capitulate to the terrorists with Morris and are horrified and deeply dissatisfied with his decision. He has given in to his fear. Yet later, as he wrestles with his shame and guilt, we realize that his reaction was completely human and understandable. He was afraid and wanted to live. We are afraid and want to live. Perhaps our fear is not the sign of weakness and failure we had thought, if even a CTU employee feels the same.

Such understanding "may help the protagonist to re-integrate emo-tionally and to process cognitively (re-cognise) his or her overwhelming loss" (Kellermann). We gain a new and expanded understanding of the fearful situation and undergo an emotional catharsis that "drain[s] the emotional residue from the trauma" (Kellermann).

In role-play, the various roles often represent different aspects of the patient's personality: "All psychodramatic techniques have the goal of mak-ing the client's internal reality overtly visible both to self and others. . . . That is, psychodramatic techniques concretize and tangibly present all aspects of the client's internal experience . . . for the purpose of increased awareness, exploration, and change" (Hudgins 32). Patients are directed to give different aspects of their personality names and to assign different peo-ple to play these roles. One patient describes her psychodrama session: "I looked at all the parts of myself on the stage. I had a wise woman, a guardian angel . . . the wounded child, the rage queen, and the controlled robot" (Hudgins 34). We all have different aspects to our personality, and understanding them can help us cope with our fears.

On 24, we are provided with such a wide range of characters, we can find one that embodies almost any aspect of our personality. Our war-rior of truth might be Jack, our manipulative self Phillip Bauer, our wise woman Karen Hayes, our greedy self Darren McCarthy, our fearful selves Marilyn Bauer and Josh, our rage queen Sherry Palmer, our guardian angel Chloe. Simply seeing these parts of ourselves expressed in con-crete form can be a powerful experience. We can recognize and accept our fear, as embodied in Marilyn Bauer. At the same time, we may real-ize that much of her fear arises from a lack of information about the sit-uation. She has turned a blind eye to her husband's activities for years. We may come to understand the negative effects of living in ignorance and take our first steps toward facing the truth of our present world. By exploring the various aspects of ourselves, we can gain confidence in our strengths and understanding of our weaknesses.

Often, patients are directed to assign someone the "perpetrator" role. A rape victim suffering from PTSD might assign someone the role of her rapist, so she can confront him and release repressed emotions. The pro-gram provides this for us as well. Through Fayed, we're able to release our repressed anger at terrorists and gain a greater understanding of the danger we face. Sometimes, a patient will even play the perpetrator role: "When clients can move in and out of the roles of perpetrators, there is a sense of mastery and reclaiming of personal power" (Hudgins 67). By experiencing the fearful event from Fayed's perspective, we reduce the feeling that we are at the mercy of forces beyond our control. When we are the terrorist, we are those forces.

Role-play sometimes involves the creation of alternate scenarios: the therapist may suggest that the patient "enact . . . what he would have liked to happen" (Kellermann). In one such case, a soldier who had failed to save his comrade role-played a situation in which he did save his friend. The purpose of role-playing alternate scenarios is not to distort reality, but to allow the patient to experience a different emotional response. This alternate response can provide a new perspective on the experience and help a patient come to terms with "an impossible outer reality through strengthening the inner subjective world of the traumatized person" (Kellermann). When the truth of our world is horrific to face, we can better cope when we have a strong internal base from which to look out upon it. This is referred to as "developmental repair" (Hudgins 58).

In the case of 24, the writers provide us with this sense of "developmental repair" as Fayed is killed and the remaining suitcase nukes are found. While the worst often happens on 24, each day ends with the specific terrorist threat conquered. Critic Douglas Winter describes the same process in horror fiction: "we control our fears, put them into order, and, more often than not, defeat them" (14). When Jack Bauer defeats the terrorists, he is providing us with an alternate scenario to September 11, one that gives us hope in what might have been and what might someday be.

As we take on various identities, role-play in 24 provides the empowering sense of knowledge, preparation, and control. Our fear transforms from a vague, overwhelming shadow to a concrete situation, and we discover which strategies are successful in coping with it and which are not. We learn what it is like to live through the aftermath of a nuclear explosion through the characters. The loss is horrific: 12,000 people killed, hospital emergency rooms overloaded, fallout drifting over the city, mass panic. Yet it is not as bad as we might have feared. A section of the city has been lost, but most of Los Angeles survives. The wind blows the radiation away from the city. The smart people get in their cars and drive. As long as they stay upwind of the radiation, they may be fine. And if we keep our heads in a similar situation, we may survive.

Our role model, Jack, does not let fear rule him. Surrounded by people running in panic, Jack stands alone, absorbing the horrific truth and preparing for action. When a helicopter pilot appeals to Jack for help, Jack snaps into action, rescuing a man trapped in the downed helicopter. Back at CTU, Chloe, Morris, Milo, and Bill Buchanan are all clearly upset by what has happened and frightened for their own safety, yet they continue to do their jobs. They are not overwhelmed by their fear, and playing their roles allows us also to avoid being overwhelmed. While aspiring to behave as Jack does may seem unrealistic, most of us find Chloe and Morris role models within our reach. If they can stay calm and cope, we gain faith that, in similar circumstances, we could do the same. We see also that there are things more important than our fear and our lives: protecting the country, maintaining our integrity, treating our loved ones well.

Assad pledges to help CTU. He retains his commitment to stop terror and broker a political settlement, despite the triumph of his enemy, despite the fact that this detonation may have ruined all chance of his success. He stays true to his beliefs.

Darren McCarthy is contacted by Fayed, who wants him to find someone to create a new trigger for the remaining nukes. His girlfriend Rita tells him he's crazy to stay. But once they capture Morris, and Rita realizes how much he's worth, she decides that staying around is worth the risk. She kills McCarthy, delivers Morris to Fayed, and demands payment. Fayed shoots her. As we experience events vicariously through them, we see that the greedy may stay and die, just as the foolish teen in a horror movie may leave the door unlocked and die, but we gain hope that we—not greedy and not foolish—may live.

Taking on the identities of those who cope poorly with their fear gives us a sense of superiority and confidence. Taking on the identities of those who cope well with the fear shows us how we might do better. This role-playing encourages us to feel that we have an understanding of the big picture and a mastery over it. Role-play makes us feel more prepared to deal with the fearful situation. It gives us confidence and hope. Whether the confidence is well-placed or not is irrelevant; it helps us to further the intellectual and emotional processing of our fearful experiences and reduce our distress.

COGNITIVE RESTRUCTURING AND RECOVERY

As we live through the consequences of nuclear fear made manifest, realize that those consequences are limited and may be survived, and that average people are capable of coping with their fears and achieving extraordinary things, our thoughts about the situation change. We undergo what psychologists would call "cognitive restructuring." This is the final stage of our PTSD therapy. We are all undergoing cognitive restructuring all the time. Any significant event leads us to compare the new information we've gained with our pre-existing knowledge and experiences. This new material may lead us to modify our beliefs. But undergoing a traumatic experience, as discussed above, may prevent us from completing this process. We may develop irrational beliefs or unhelpful patterns of thinking about terrorists, ourselves, and our world. In PTSD therapy, "cognitive restructuring enables a person to identify negative, irrational beliefs having to do with a psychological trauma and to replace them with truthful, rational beliefs" (Arehart-Treichel 21). To consider what sort of restructuring the terrorist attacks of September 11 caused, let's first consider what beliefs we might have held on September 10.

Psychologist Seymour Epstein suggests that many people, prior to a trauma, hold four core beliefs: "the belief that the world is benign, that the world is meaningful, that the self is worthy, and that people are trustworthy" (qtd. in Foa). In many of us, these core beliefs were shaken by the trauma of September 11. The world certainly no longer seems benign, and with people killed randomly and with no warning, the world no longer seems meaningful. While the self may still seem worthy, others may be viewed with suspicion or fear.

With these core beliefs in doubt, what are some of the irrational beliefs or unhelpful thought patterns that may have developed since 9/11? How do we now think of ourselves and our world? Psychologist Leah Giarratano suggests common beliefs of PTSD sufferers include, "'I'm helpless.' 'I'm going to die.' 'I'm exposed.' 'I'm not safe anywhere anymore.' 'I'm weak'" (Giarratano 260). Fears of terrorism may encourage additional beliefs: My family is in danger. Flying is not safe. Cities are not safe. I have no control. Nothing is certain. Others are not what they seem. Terrorists are going to destroy us. The end of Western civilization is coming. The world has permanently changed for the worse. We will never be the same. We will never be safe. Psychiatrist Edna Foa suggests that many of these beliefs boil down to one: "The world is completely dangerous" (Foa).

Our original core beliefs stand in conflict with these new beliefs, and we require cognitive restructuring to reconcile them. This process can help us to "integrate the conflicting information and to construct new meanings of the old and the new" (Kellermann). Creating these new meanings allows us to make a "journey of readjustment to the new reality . . . to make sense of a world that has momentarily lost structure and meaning" (Kellermann). It may seem impossible to develop a rational worldview in these dangerous, unpredictable times, but we need to find a new way to think about the world, one in which we are not overwhelmed by fear; cognitive restructuring helps us "direct [our] efforts at changing these disturbing thoughts" (Giarratano 114).

As we turn off the television at the end of another great episode of *24*, we leave the world of Jack Bauer and return to the real world. Because we have been away, living in the fictional world, the real world seems slightly different to us when we return—just as it does when we return from a vacation. J. R. R. Tolkien calls this process "recovery" and defines it as "a re-gaining—regaining of a clear view" (57). We see our world anew, almost as if we're seeing it for the first time. The more vivid and striking the fictional world was, the stronger the experience of recovery. We have gained a new perspective on our lives.

The fact that *24* helps trigger this cognitive restructuring does not mean that we believe everything on the show is real, or even realistic. But watching *24* has been an emotional and intellectual experience, resonating deep within our traumatized selves. Through exposure, the show has helped us process our emotions. Through role-play, it has given us confidence and a greater sense of control. And after these experiences, we move ahead in the restructuring of our thoughts and beliefs. We feel less fear at the terrorist threats we face. Danger exists, but it is limited. We have a better sense that, while some situations may leave us helpless, there are many situations in which we can play a key role, in which we can change events. Even if we sometimes fail or capitulate, we can still be strong, admirable, and honorable people. And we see that others may help us—even others who are Muslims. We are not alone. The world is not entirely dangerous. The world has changed, yes, but some things survive: courage, commitment, and heroism, in us and those around us. Our country survives. And as long as average people stand up for their beliefs and don't succumb to fear, we can prevail. Cognitive restructuring has occurred; we have a new perspective.

OUR BRAVE NEW WORLD

With the help of 24, we've received treatment for many of our terrorism-related fears: fear of biological attack, fear of chemical attack, fear of an attack on our nuclear power plants, fear of having our own weapons turned against us, fear of losing our rights if our government overreacts, fear of losing control to the military-industrial complex, fear of terrorists in our midst, and more. We are now more habituated to a world with terrorism. In fact, our world almost seems tame compared to what Jack Bauer has to face each day. After living through those extreme situations, our lives don't seem so bad, because now we understand that "things could, after all, be worse" (Winter 13).

While 24 offers its viewers many pleasures and rewards, one of the most valuable may be its weekly treatment for PTSD. The program allows us—amidst chills, twists, romance, and thrills—to overcome the avoidance that is at the heart of PTSD and to work through the trauma, fear, and disturbing beliefs that have haunted us since September 11. We process our distress emotionally and intellectually, and find a new way to live in our new world. We face the horrors with clear eyes and accept them, and we gain confidence in our ability to cope—to face our world and whatever may come. Helping us cope with fears of terrorism, when we hear new threats every day, is a far more difficult task than soothing fears of nonexistent homicidal maniacs or distant missiles sitting silent for decades. But if anyone can accomplish the task, it would be Jack Bauer.

JEANNE CAVELOS began her professional life as an astrophysicist, working in the Astronaut Training Division at NASA's Johnson Space Center. After earning her MFA in creative writing, she moved into a career in publishing, becoming a senior editor at Bantam Doubleday Dell, where she created and launched the Abyss imprint of psychological horror, for which she won the World Fantasy Award, and ran the science fiction/fantasy publishing program. Jeanne left New York to pursue her own writing career. Her books include the best-selling Passing of the Techno-Mages trilogy, the highly praised science books *The Science of Star Wars* and *The Science of The X-Files*, and the anthology *The Many Faces of Van Helsing*. Her work has twice been nominated for the Bram Stoker Award. Jeanne is currently at work on a thriller about genetic manipulation, titled *Fatal Spiral*. Jeanne created and serves as director of Odyssey, an annual six-week summer workshop for writers of science fiction, fantasy, and horror held at Saint Anselm College in Manchester, New Hampshire. Guest lecturers have included George R. R. Martin, Harlan Ellison, Terry Books, Jane Yolen, and Dan Simmons. More information about Jeanne is on her Web site, www.jeannecavelos.com.

REFERENCES

Arehart-Treichel, Joan. "Data Back Cognitive-Behavior Therapy for PTSD Treatment." *Psychiatric News* 36.23 (2001): 21.

Badkhen, Anna. "Al Qaeda Bluffing About Having Suitcase Nukes, Experts Say; Russians Claim Terrorists Couldn't Have Bought Them." *San Francisco Chronicle*, 23 Mar. 2004, final ed.: A8.

Broad, William J., Stephen Engelberg, and James Glanz. "A Nation Challenged: The Threats; Assessing Risks, Chemical, Biological, Even Nuclear." *New York Times*. 1 Nov. 2001, late ed. final: A1.

Clancy, Tom. *The Sum of All Fears*. New York: Berkley, 2002.

"Epidemiology." American Psychiatric Association Web site. 2006. <http://www.psych.org/disaster/dpc_epidemiology.cfm>

Foa, Edna B., et al. "The Posttraumatic Cognitions Inventory (PTCI): Development and Validation." *Psychological Assessment* 11.3 (1999): 303–314. EBSCOhost Research Database. 18 May 2007. <http://search.epnet.com>

Giarratano, Leah. *Clinical Skills for Treating Traumatised Adolescents.* Mascot, Australia: Talomin Books, 2004.

Glazer, Sarah. "Treating Anxiety." *CQ Researcher* 12 (2002): 97–120. CQ Researcher Online 13 May 2007. <http://0-library.cqpress.com. library.anselm.edu:80/cqresearcher/cqresrre2002020800>

Green, Frank. "Fears of Terror Add Up; Latest Alert Means Higher Sales, Profits for Some." *San Diego Union-Tribune*, 20 Feb. 2003: C1.

Hudgins, M. Katherine. *Experiential Treatment for PTSD: The Therapeutic Spiral Model.* New York: Springer Publishing, 2002.

Keinan, Giora, Avi Sadeh, and Sefi Rosen. "Attitudes and Reactions to Media Coverage of Terrorist Acts." *Journal of Community Psychology* 31.2 (2003): 149–165.

Keller, Bill. "Nuclear Nightmares." *New York Times Magazine* 26 May 2002, late ed. final: 22.

Kellermann, Peter Felix. "The Therapeutic Aspects of Psychodrama with Traumatised People." Soul's Self-Help Central. 2000. <http://www.soulselfhelp.on.ca/d2.html>

Studio B. FoxNews. 8 May 2007.

Tolkien, J. R. R. "On Fairy-Stories." *Tree and Leaf.* New York: Houghton Mifflin, 1965. 3–73.

United States. Department of Veterans Affairs. "National Center for Treatment of PTSD Fact Sheet: Treatment of PTSD." National Center for Posttraumatic Stress Disorder Web site. 6 Apr. 2007. <http://www.ncptsd.va.gov/ncmain/ ncdocs/ fact_shts/fs_treatmentforptsd.html>

Webster, Philip, and Roland Watson. "Bin Laden's Nuclear Threat: Detention of Top Pakistani Atomic Scientists Heightens Fear al-Qaeda Has Nuclear Material." *Ottawa Citizen* 26 Oct. 2001, early ed.: A1.

Wilson, Edmund. *A Literary Chronicle: 1920-1950.* New York: Doubleday, 1956.

Winter, Douglas E., ed. *Prime Evil.* New York: Signet Books, 1989.

Can a Leftist Love 24?

STEVEN RUBIO

In 1974, *Ms.* magazine asked, "Can a Feminist Love the World's Greatest Rock Band?" The band was the Rolling Stones, who had earned their "Greatest" sobriquet for songs like "Under My Thumb" and "Starfucker." That a band that arguably *was* the greatest could be reduced to any one specific malfeasance seems a bit simplistic, but the sentiment behind the article's title was understandable. How do we evaluate art when that art involves itself in areas we find problematic? How do we respond when the art doesn't agree with our notions of what is *proper*? How *does* a feminist look herself in the mirror, when she loves the Rolling Stones?

This is not a unique question. Popular culture often simultaneously enthralls us and posits a disagreeable worldview. The better the work is, the more it enthralls, and the more guilty we feel about our enjoyment.

Liberals and others of a more leftist bent have special reason to be concerned. Most pop culture action movies feature a hero (or, less often, a heroine) who fights a lone battle against a chaotic universe of bad guys and gals, doing the dirty work for which the rest of us are unsuited, saving society from destruction. There is no reason why these heroes must

19

have a conservative political philosophy; there is no reason for these heroes to have any explicit politics at all. Some interpret the work of action stars like John Wayne or Clint Eastwood as reactionary, even fascist, but the left wing has its heroes, too. Granted, Steven Seagal isn't quite the screen presence that Clint or the Duke are. But in Seagal's very first film, *Above the Law*, the CIA were bad guys, and after *Under Siege* brought home more than $150 million, Big Steve's vanity-project follow-up, *On Deadly Ground*, which he produced, directed, and starred in, told the story of an evil oil company stopped by an environmentalist who also kicks ass.

Seagal was only channeling the original Ass-Kicker for Peace, Tom Laughlin's Billy Jack, who spent four movies making the world safe for peace-loving people like Native Americans and kids in free schools by using karate on the bad guys.

But despite the attempts at left-wing politics, movies by people like Seagal and Laughlin end up reinforcing the values inherent in this type of action adventure. If society must rely on a savior, if we can't solve our problems and defeat our enemies collectively but must instead ask the hero to make our world safe, then we are accepting the validity of the cult of individualism that makes heroes like those played by John Wayne and Clint Eastwood possible. Steve Seagal can make as many Chomsky-esque speeches in as many movies as he wants; the movies still propose the hero as savior. The glorification of the superhero is just as fascist in a "liberal" movie as it is in a "conservative" movie. The question of the movie's politics is tangential to the real point, which argues that heroic individualism is what makes us great. And that point runs counter to the collective spirit of leftist thought, which, it would seem, makes it impossible for action adventures to be both enthralling and "liberal."

A brief explanation of my use of the terms "individualism" and "collectivism" in the context of conservative and liberal American politics is in order. I would argue that individualism tends to be associated with conservative America. The idea that America is a place where a person can be anything and anyone, combined with a preference for limited government, connects the stalwart individual hero of American myth and history with a more conservative philosophy. Collectivism, often reduced in American discourse to an argument over socialist interventions into government, exists in a somewhat watered-down mode as a combination of a larger governmental intervention into the lives of Americans, in order to benefit them as a group, and what might be called the *isms* of modern culture, where individuals acquire identity through their connection to particular groups. The statement "I am a feminist" does not promote individuality, but rather associates the speaker with an identifiable group. Thus, one would think that, to the extent there is such a thing as "liberal" culture, it would be a culture that valued collectivism. But the long-lasting prevalence of the myth of the lone American hero is apparently too strong, so that even so-called liberal culture eventually allies itself with the heroic individual rather than the heroic community.

Which leads us to *24*. A lot of people like watching Jack Bauer. Many of those fans are unapologetic. But then there are the liberal and leftist fans of the show who like the roller-coaster excitement, but are appalled by the perceived reactionary nature of the series's politics. My argument here is that they are worried about the wrong thing. It's not *24*'s stance on terrorism or torture that should concern liberals; it's *24*'s stance on the usefulness of heroic individualism that matters. Does *24* valorize Jack Bauer? Can a leftist love the world's greatest action TV show?

But first. . . .

LET'S TALK ABOUT TORTURE

Everyone else does.

In *Raw*, Eddie Murphy talks about being chastised by Bill Cosby for including "filth, flarn, filth" in his act. "I got mad," says Eddie, "cuz he thought that was my whole act. Like I just walked out on stage and cursed and left. And I manage to stick in some jokes between the curses, you couldn't give no curse show." Torture is the curse of *24*. The central premise of the series, that each season takes place over the course of twenty-four hours while a clock ticks on screen, was easily the most revolutionary part of the show at the beginning. But that premise is mostly taken for granted at this point. What gets people talking are the scenes of torture, and our internal Cosby can be very bothered by what seems on the surface to be an endorsement of the tactical use of torture to elicit information. Beyond the personal discomfort such scenes might cause, is there reason to believe that *24*'s torture scenes have not only a personal but a socially negative impact?

I'm not referring here to the notion that violence in popular culture can lead to emulation by individuals in the real world. Rather, I'm talking about the concern that we might become anesthetized to torture, or that there is a danger that 24 is making a case for the use of torture in the real world to solve real-world problems. Or even a combination of the two, so that those in power might be more likely to use torture and we might be more acquiescent in its use.

I would suggest that, even if what drives people's discomfort is their personal, visceral reaction to the torture scenes, their arguments focus on the social and political ramifications. This holds true not only for viewers, but for those involved in the making of the show, whether they are anti-torture or . . . it is unfair to say *pro-torture*, so let's just say less concerned about the use of torture on the series. In a now-famous article in the *New Yorker*, series writer Howard Gordon, a "moderate Democrat," said that "nobody wants to be the handmaid to a relaxed policy that accepts torture as a legitimate means of interrogation," while star Kiefer Sutherland expressed qualms about the "unintended consequences of the show" (Mayer). In both cases, the impact of 24's torture scenes in a larger social context is seen as the problem. (Mention is often made that Sutherland is the grandson of Tommy Douglas, a renowned socialist politician from Canada, as if the connection between the left-wing politician and the actor is an important fact when analyzing the television series.)

It is also argued that 24 overstates the efficacy of torture as a method for extracting information. Again from the *New Yorker*:

> U.S. Army Brigadier General Patrick Finnegan, the dean of the United States Military Academy at West Point, flew to Southern California to meet with the creative team . . . to voice their concern that the show's central political premise — that the letter of American law must be sacrificed for the country's security — was having a toxic effect. In their view, the show promoted unethical and illegal behavior and had adversely affected the training and performance of real American soldiers. "I'd like them to stop," Finnegan said of the show's producers. "They should do a show where torture

backfires." . . . Finnegan told the producers that *24*, by suggesting that the U.S. government perpetrates myriad forms of
torture, hurts the country's image internationally. (Mayer)

Finnegan not only questioned the actual use of torture in specific situations, but also assumed that the fictional (and successful) torture in *24*
had real-life international implications.

    All of this causes consternation among viewers of the series who don't
want to be seen as enjoying torture as entertainment. It would appear
that leftist fans of the show are doubly tormented; not only are they worried about torture, they feel a fundamental disparity between their politics and what they perceive as the politics of *24*. Jon Carroll, writing in
the *San Francisco Chronicle*, answered his own question when he wrote,
"How can I justify watching a right-wing wet dream television program?
I can't, actually." (Which doesn't stop him from watching, nonetheless.)
"Freshair2" offered one of the best explanations of this quandary in a
post on the progressive blog "The Daily Kos" titled "The Guiltiest of
Pleasures": "[T]he greatest right-wing propaganda show ever made . . .
if you can manage to let go of the fact that it represents everything you
hate and despise in the world, *24* is a blast."

    The joy that freshair2 experiences points to something crucial: the
show is a blast. Whether or not *24* accurately portrays the real-world
effects of torture (and given the show's almost complete implausibility on
nearly every level, it's not clear why anyone would single out torture as
the one area where authenticity is required), what ultimately matters is
whether or not torture works as a dramatic device. And the powers
behind *24* clearly think that it works just fine. Joel Surnow, the executive
producer of the show and the primary focus of the *New Yorker* article,
may preen about how popular his show is with conservatives and brag
about how "patriotic" his show is, but what he is really concerned with
is much more elemental. In the context of the "ticking clock" scenario,
torture scenes ratchet up the excitement level, contributing to the edge-
of-your-seat feeling that makes the series popular. Howard Gordon
admits that "the *premise* of *24* is the ticking time bomb. It takes an unusual situation and turns it into the meat and potatoes of the show," adding,
"I think people can differentiate between a television show and reality"
(Mayer). (When the frequency of torture scenes lessened midway

through season six, it was because they were losing their effectiveness as drama through overuse, Gordon indicated, not because Surnow suddenly had a change of heart.)

In much of this, leftist fans of the show seem to conflate conservative politics with torture, as if they could assuage their guilt over taking pleasure from 24 by telling themselves that the worst actions of Jack Bauer and his team are mere reflections of the reactionary militarism they hate so much in real life. But as I argued earlier, any attempt to critique 24 by simply connecting it to specific social concerns is misdirected, for no matter the "politics" of Jack Bauer, his existence as a heroic individual who saves society gives the lie to surface political analysis. In the end, whether or not Jack Bauer uses torture effectively, whether or not 24 is popular with conservatives or liberals, what 24 offers is a fairly standard model of heroic individualism—one that rejects communal action in favor of something quite similar to what John Wayne and Clint Eastwood offer as icons. And as everyone from Steven Seagal to Billy Jack show us, there is no way around this conundrum, outside of creating a new model for heroism that is communal. (Some would point to Jack's compatriots at CTU as evidence of a communal activism, but in fact, the series is constructed so that CTU and other government agencies obstruct Jack just as much as do supposed do-gooder ACLU-style liberals. Only when Jack, acting alone, solicits the personal assistance of a Chloe or a David Palmer does anyone truly help Jack. He remains the one person who can get the job done.)

I have tried so far to show that the guilt leftists feel for enjoying 24, while understandable, leads to analysis of peripheral issues rather than the core of what 24 represents. And an obsession with torture, to which all of us eventually fall victim, is the 24 version of filth, flarn, and filth: they manage to stick in some excitement between the torture scenes; you can't just do a torture show. But up to now I have accepted the terms of the discussion—that in some ways, 24 reflects contemporary society, and that our personal politics affect how we react to the series, resulting in our feeling a need to do back flips when our politics conflict with those we think the show is proposing. I asked if a leftist can love 24, and I haven't exactly answered the question. I've given examples of leftists who do love the show, which is something of an answer, I suppose, and I've discussed how complicated that love can make one's life. What I haven't done yet, what needs to be done, is to contest the actual assumptions of the question itself. Why are we even asking if a leftist can love 24? What does that question really mean?

IT's ALL WE'VE GOT

There is a rather persistent notion that we should support art, no matter how crummy, if it meets our preconceived notions of what is necessary in the socio-cultural arena. A good example of this in contemporary television is *The L Word*, a mediocre show where we are supposed to restrain ourselves from commenting on its weaknesses because, as one person argued on *Television Without Pity*, "[I]t's the only full on lesbian show we've got," adding, "maybe we could show a little restraint on the pedantic nitpicking and character hostility and more support instead. The blatant negativity isn't likely to help the show in any useful way." It's clear the creators of *The L Word* are counting on this. No matter how bad the show gets, we're supposed to be grateful it exists at all. Art is being evaluated more on its "proper" cultural position than on its quality as a work of art. How many people became Dixie Chicks fans not because they fell in love with the music, but because they fell in love with that lady who dissed George W. Bush? Just as a lot of people decided then and there that they no longer liked the Dixie Chicks's music because of their political views, there were people who decided to buy some Dixie Chicks albums to show their support for free speech. Free speech is a great thing, and Dixie Chicks albums are good things, but it might be better if people were buying Dixie Chicks albums because they thought the albums were good instead of buying them because Natalie Maines said a mean thing about Bush. Deciding you like the Dixie Chicks because of what Maines said is just as stupid as deciding you don't like them for the same reason.

One needs to be wary of this kind of logic, which applies in particular to the case of 24. Whatever conflicts a viewer might have with the show based on the politics they bring to the table can only interfere with a useful analysis of the art of the series. It is, of course, perfectly legitimate to judge works on the basis of our agreement or disagreement with the perceived politics of the work in question. It is likely unavoidable that such concerns enter into our feelings about the work. Part of what makes us like or dislike a work of art is the extent to which we "agree" with it, or it agrees with us. But it is one thing to say "we need more full-on lesbian television shows," and another to say "therefore, *The L Word* is high-quality TV." It is one thing to want popular culture that better reflects who we are as a diverse populace, and another to say that we should turn off our critical faculties in the name of supporting something that has more cultural importance than it does artistic value. And it is one thing to have concerns about the use of torture on *24*, and another to say that *24* is bad art because it features scenes of torture. It might be more dangerous art, but the cultural impact does not necessarily change the aesthetics.

I am not trying to make a case against close readings of popular cultural texts. But neither do I think it useful to reject a text because we don't like its implications. Ruthless criticism is a good thing, but the words of Emma Goldman also hold true: If you can't dance, what's the point of the revolution? The need to analyze popular culture for what it tells us about our greater culture is crucial. But we shouldn't be afraid to like something. The question isn't whether a leftist can love *24*, the question is whether ANYONE can love *24*. An understanding of the larger implications of the series should not prevent us from pleasure. The answer to the question is, yes, a leftist can love *24* just as anyone can. Or can't.

In Eddie Murphy's Cosby anecdote in *Raw*, he admits to being frustrated and offended. So he calls Richard Pryor on the telephone. Richard advises Eddie, "Whatever the fuck makes the people laugh, say that shit. Do the people laugh when you say what you say? Do you get paid? Well, tell Bill I said have a Coke and a smile and shut the fuck up."

CONSEQUENCES

None of this lets *24* off the hook. There is a reason why fans, left and right, can finally give in to their pleasures and ignore the horrors of torture (and nuclear bombs going off, assassinations, and everything else that occurs on the show). On *24*, actions lack real consequences.

This is obvious in three ways. First, the big picture. Season six begins with a nuclear bomb going off in Southern California. As a plot device, this works very well. But the consequences are all related to narrative. The bomb sets the season's plot in motion. The actual victims of the bomb are almost completely forgotten as the season progresses (and since the structure of the series demands that fewer than twenty-four hours have passed since the bomb was detonated, the forgetting takes remarkably little time). Even when a beloved politician is assassinated, he's not really dead. David Palmer goes to the grave, only to have his brother win a subsequent election, ensuring that "President Palmer" survives.

Neither does physical trauma have lasting consequences, a matter of particular import when it comes to torture. Many jokes have been made about the absence of potty trips for Jack and his crew, but a full bladder is hardly the worst thing to be swept under the rug on *24*. Every season features people being shot, stabbed, tortured, even caught in a lion trap, only to find those same people hard at work only hours later. The case of Morris O'Brian in season six is as good an example as any. Sometime around 1:40 P.M., after being clubbed in the head and being held under water, Morris's suffering reached a peak when a terrorist took a power drill to his shoulder. An hour later, he was being asked to start back to work at CTU. Which he did. Not that Morris was no longer suffering— he has bouts of self-doubt mixed between spats with his ex-wife.

Most important of all, there is a significant lack of emotional consequences. There are clear attempts throughout the history of *24* to show the consequences of Jack Bauer's actions on his own well-being. We are constantly being led to believe that Jack suffers inwardly from the actions he must perform in the service of his country. At the end of season three, Jack finally burst into tears as the accumulation of a thousand hours finally broke him down. And then? Back to work. Twenty months of torture? No problem. Wife murdered? Kill the killer and move on. Jack just keeps on ticking.

If anyone believes that these examples prove that Jack suffers, I would point them to shows with more depth that give us real consequences. Vic Mackey on *The Shield* lives a life at least as brutal as Jack Bauer's. Mackey killed a fellow cop in cold blood in the very first episode of the series. He has Jack's flair for original, creative torture techniques. He believes he is saving the world from ugliness, and that therefore the ends justify the means. He does things he knows are "wrong" because in the big picture they are "right."

The Shield differs from *24*, though, in how Vic's actions have real consequences. His murder of a cop is slowly but inexorably putting the squeeze on Vic. He recognizes, and we in the audience see, that the brutality of his job is making him more brutal. We are even given visual reminders. At one point in an early season, Vic interrogated a suspect by pushing his face down on an active electric stove. Later, the bad guys retaliated by doing the same to one of Vic's partners. For several seasons the character sported a beard, always there to remind us of what it covered. And when, some years later, he finally shaved off the facial hair, we could see the spiral burn marks still on his cheek. *The Shield* never lets anyone forget.

Yet forgetting is what *24* is all about. The violence, and the aftermath of that violence, is no more real than that seen in a Road Runner cartoon.

This ability to forget is what makes *24* tolerable, no matter the political perspective of the viewer. And I would return to an earlier point, that the real issue with *24* isn't about torture or politics, left or right, but rather with its valorization of heroic individualism, a process that goes unquestioned. While *24* is great at putting us on the edge of our seats, it is unconcerned with any real examination of the true nature of our love affair with the hero, or rather, it sees no need for such an examination because it happily participates in that love affair. That Jack Bauer is a hero goes without question. That we root for him to succeed is clear. But the obsession with torture scenes and conservative politics deflects our analysis away from the one area where I would argue that *24* falls short as art. For *24* to raise itself to that level, things need to matter. But when you are required to crank up the machinery once again the following week, you can't spend time on consequences. There is always another bomb, another terrorist, another job that needs to be done by our hero, Jack Bauer.

STEVEN RUBIO has never been cornered by a mountain lion. His writing has been featured in several books in the Smart Pop series.

REFERENCES

Mayer, Jane. "Whatever It Takes." *The New Yorker*. 19 Feb. 2007.

"I Despise You for Making Me Do This"

Evaluating Jack Bauer's Use of Violence for the Greater Good

BRETT CHANDLER PATTERSON

Imagine that terrorists have smuggled a nuclear bomb into an American city and that the bomb is set to explode in a few hours. Agents under your command have captured the mastermind and brought him to you for interrogation. As you walk into the room where the suspect is restrained, you are aware that the minutes are ticking by and that millions of lives are on the line. You approach the suspect, noting the grim resistance in his face. What do you do next? This compelling, yet nightmarish, scenario often arises in university ethics courses, where a safe distance gives time to reflect, but it also appears repeatedly on the television show *24*, where viewers encounter these issues more viscerally. Most often it is Jack Bauer in these interrogation sequences, deciding that he must use torture to get the necessary information out of the person in question. Torture is just one among several violent tactics Jack Bauer has used to combat the chaos that terrorism threatens to unleash on our society. However, *24* emphasizes that Jack Bauer does not approach the use of violence eagerly or casually; he feels that he must do whatever is necessary to stop these large-scale threats, that his opponents have forced his hand and that he does not have any choice but to respond in kind. What toll does Jack pay, though, for taking such actions? Jack sacrifices much in his engagements with terrorists. There have been significant points, however, at which he has doubted whether what he has achieved has been worth what he has lost. As we explore Jack's world, we ask similar questions of ourselves and our social order. Do we condone the use of violence against suspected terrorists? Is torture inevitable in these situations? And what is its cost?

In an ethics class, the ticking-bomb scenario often arises to explain an age-old debate between those who perceive morality primarily in terms of laws that govern our actions and those who perceive morality primarily in terms of the goals that we seek in our actions. Here we must evaluate what grounds our understandings of what is good and bad, what is admirable and reprehensible, what comprises a moral life or a life of vice and villainy. Philosophical ethics textbooks often highlight two major traditions, corresponding to these two different perspectives, which locate the foundations of the moral life either in actions themselves (actions are inherently moral or immoral) or in the intended consequences of actions (actions are moral if the agent has moral intentions). Ethics respectively becomes either a discussion of which parameters should be placed upon our actions or a debate over which consequences are preferable. Law-based (deontological) perspectives, often associated with the Enlightenment philosopher Immanuel Kant, ask what rules govern our actions in a given situation. In this case, they would suggest that the United States has agreed to certain international laws that forbid the use of torture, seeing the action itself as abhorrent. On the other hand, goal-based (teleological) perspectives, instead weigh the consequences of not torturing (the almost guaranteed loss of millions of lives) with the consequences of torturing (the increased chance of locating and stopping the bomb). This latter reasoning is most associated with the utilitarian philosophers Jeremy Bentham and John Stuart Mill, and has become popularized in the sayings, "The ends justify the means," and "The greatest good for the greatest number." The ticking-bomb scenario is often mentioned in the debate between these two schools of thought; it is an emotional scenario and seems inherently weighted toward the utilitarians. How could one not choose to inflict pain on someone who aims to be a mass murderer in order to raise the chance of saving the lives of millions of innocents? Has he not brought this upon himself?

The answer seems a foregone conclusion. Yet there remain some people who think that torture is an evil action and that resorting to it is to violate the very standards that the United States is based on.

And there are still others who adopt a third perspective. One of the more important voices here, H. Richard Niebuhr (drawing from a tradition that includes, among others, Aristotle and Aquinas) wrote in *The Responsible Self* that we should attend to the person who is making the decision before we focus on the action itself or the intended consequences. The moral life encompasses actions and consequences, but even more primary is the person who is trying to live a moral life. We should shift our concern to how people first interpret and describe what is going on. Interpretation arises from the application of a language, and a language arises from a communal context. We should seek to understand what community or communities have helped to shape the point of view of this individual and what values, virtues, or vices guide the person in making a decision. The overall shape of that person's life frequently is communicated through a narrative; people make choices based upon what kind of person they want to be, what kind of character they possess. If we are to follow the trajectory suggested by Niebuhr in our analysis of Jack Bauer's use of violence, we should widen our focus and pull back from the choices made in the interrogation room to look at the entire outline of Jack's life, giving special attention to the source of his values and the shape of his character. To comment on his actions, we must consider who Jack Bauer is and who he seeks to be.

WHO IS JACK BAUER?

It may be impossible for us to get a working understanding of the outline of Jack's life because of the very nature of the show—we see only twenty-four-hour snapshots. Even though the show has been around for six seasons at the writing of this essay, we only have six days with which to evaluate Jack's character! I would hazard to say that most people would not want to be judged entirely by their actions in such a limited sampling. Yet if you were given the chance to pick six of the most important days in your life, would you reconsider? I am not sure whether Jack Bauer would have chosen these exact days himself, but the writers of *24* have chosen to portray these days because they are crucially important

31

days for the fictional representation of the United States and they do reveal Jack's heroism as he faces such horrors. These six days are not any old ordinary days; they are phenomenally bad days (pushing the plausibility factor for some viewers). The show bases its very existence upon elaborate, complex events that place Jack (or push Jack into placing himself) in a myriad of rushed tortuous situations. Popular belief often espouses that we learn who people really are when they are under pressure, and there is certainly stress enough on 24 to claim that we are seeing Jack reveal his true mettle.

In these six days, Jack Bauer displays a character that grows out of a series of commitments, most notably to his country and to his family. Jack's perspective, like our belief systems, largely arises from participation in these communities. In a community we share a common vision, trusting in the value of that vision and those who share it; we in turn show loyalty to that vision and those people. Participation in the life of the community involves the implementation of, or rebellion against, that community's web of value relationships. Because Jack Bauer is loyal to the U.S. government and shares the liberal values described in the Constitution and promoted in current U.S. political theory, he has learned to evaluate the efforts of other governments through the system of values that makes up American society.

We, of course, may belong to more than one community, each community with its own web of values, and therefore life often becomes the juggling and clashing of different value systems.[1] Because we viewers have not been given a sense of how Jack grew into the man that he is, what kind of family life he had as a youth, or what kind of training he received to become a CTU agent, we cannot trace how Jack reasoned himself into his current responsibilities, but we can observe the way he relates to his family, his fellow federal employees, and his enemies. In the days dramatized on 24, we see Jack caught in the midst of conflict between his commitments, most notably those to his family and to his country.

We learn some important things about Jack in the chaos that is 24. We learn that Jack values family, for he is constantly reaching out to them and trying to justify his vocational choices to them even as he is in the

---

[1] Here I am again drawing from the work of H. Richard Niebuhr. See particularly *Faith on Earth* (48-51), *Radical Monotheism and Western Culture* (11-15 and 109-110), and *Christ and Culture* (38-39).

middle of foiling the terrorist plots. *24* is never just about the terrorist stories; it is also about the family drama. When season one introduced us to Jack Bauer, he was in the midst of a domestic discussion with his daughter and then with his wife. Jack was trying to negotiate how to hold his family together, a task made difficult because of his rebellious teenage daughter and a recently ended estrangement from his wife. Throughout the season, Jack fought to pull his wife and daughter out of jeopardy, and the loss of his wife at the end of that season was the heaviest of blows. Afterward, he turned his back on CTU, but events in the next season pulled him back in. Seasons two and three showed Jack struggling to stay in contact with his daughter while trying to keep terrorist plots from hurting millions of others—and there was also the promise of a connection with Kate Warner. After being fired for being too much of a loose cannon, Jack left CTU again, this time for the Department of Defense, where he met Audrey Raines, who became the new love interest for seasons four, five, and six. Since Audrey was missing for most of season six, the writers introduced (sister-in-law) Marilyn and (nephew) Josh Bauer to give Jack visible family ties. Jack's job constantly has interfered with his important relationships—dramatically demonstrated by Audrey's roller-coaster response during season four and in Jack's fight with Senator Heller over Audrey's fate at the end of season six. Jack wants to have a life outside of CTU; he longs for the intimacy of these relationships.

Yet Jack has also obviously committed himself to his country. Jack works for a counterterrorism unit in Los Angeles, a government agency that ultimately reports to the president of the United States. Jack works to protect the American government and the American people. Jack also belongs to the community that is CTU. He counts Tony, Michelle, Chloe, Curtis, and others as friends.[2] Jack admires the contributions of others who also seek to uphold the United States—the most important relationship here has been the one between Jack and President Palmer. Jack has stated that it was an honor to serve under him, and it was Palmer's record that contributed to Jack's disgust with President Logan in season

---

[2] This commitment to friendship made the killing of Chappell in season three and Curtis in season six such horrific moments. Jack declared after shooting Curtis that he was done forever with field work, but of course when the nuclear bomb detonated, he felt that he had no choice but to resume the war.

five. Logan corrupted himself, thereby endangering the country he served, and Jack did all that was in his power to expose the man, even if he was the president.

Closely associated with Jack's devotion to the United States is his steadfast commitment to his values. Early in season one Jack told Nina that he exposed three fellow agents because they compromised CTU principles; Jack wanted to make sure that he and Nina did not do the same thing. (The irony was that Nina had already compromised herself and CTU to a degree that Jack would discover too late). Jack wants to ensure that others know that he would never do anything that would compromise the people of the United States. His job is to protect them; he will not betray them.

But Jack's job puts his family and friends at risk, and they become a "weakness" that his enemies can exploit. Season one hinted at previous covert operations that had taken Jack into other countries; these assignments created the ill will among the Drazens that fueled that season's attack on Jack's family. Jack constantly seeks to balance being a husband, father, lover, and friend with his vision of loyalty to his country. But there are times when he cannot be in both places at once, when he cannot serve the interests of friends and family at the same time as those of his country; a sacrifice must be made. When backed into a corner, Jack sacrifices his family and friends, and in so doing, sacrifices his dreams for himself.

In season three, when talking to Chase—a younger agent paired to work with him—about Chase's relationship with his daughter Kim, Jack clearly stated that he knew that field agents could not have healthy family lives. One wonders whether Jack was being a little hypocritical here, given his own continued longing for family and friends, or whether he was just trying to keep Chase, and more importantly Kim, from a life as miserable as his had been. Jack here was certainly speaking from personal experience. And there were more personal/professional catch-22 situations to come.

In season four, Jack tortured Audrey's estranged husband Paul and then later made the decision to pull CTU's one doctor away from saving Paul's life to work on saving a suspect who could help them stop a nuclear missile from hitting an American city. The choice led to Paul's death and Audrey's pulling away. In season six, wrestling with their betrayals, Jack tortured his brother for information and later left his father (apparently) to die on an oil rig that had been targeted for an air strike. But despite these dark moments, Jack is always trying to right the balance. He takes any moment that he can to call his loved ones, and he makes sacrifices trying to save them.

In this constant juggling of commitments, we see that Jack is ingenious, tenacious, and trustworthy. He has high standards of honor and loyalty and loathes those who betray him, CTU, and the American people. He seeks to preserve the lives of his fellow agents and those civilians caught up in terrorist plots whenever possible, but he is willing to put these people in dangerous positions whenever necessary to draw out information that could lead to capturing the terrorists or foiling their violence.

Such logic should look familiar. In many ways Jack appears to be the prototypical utilitarian; he is looking for the greatest good for the greatest number of people. Yet, this characterization alone is too simplistic. At the end of season six, in arguing that he needs to save his nephew Josh just because he is an innocent, Jack looks much more like a rule-based (deontological) thinker opposing the heartless utilitarians in the White House. The responsible-self model, which calls us to give attention to the shape of Jack's life, helps us to see that Jack is trying to balance the commitments to these two communities—his country and his family. Jack feels that he must sacrifice for the greater good in his efforts to stop terrorists; his logic is utilitarian. But when he turns back to his family, he realizes that his longing for intimacy and his sense of loyalty prevents him from being a complete utilitarian all of the time. Of course, there have been heart-wrenching moments when Jack has sacrificed friends and family, because forces were beyond his control or because he felt that there was no other way, but these moments are torturous to Jack, enough so that he often gives up on the CTU job. Incredible circumstances just keep pulling him back in.

I DESPISE YOU FOR MAKING ME DO THIS:
THE LOGIC OF A UTILITARIAN MARTYR

How does the logic of a utilitarian martyr work? Utilitarian logic often supports a just-war perspective: We are justified in using violence, in waging war on those who threaten us, but we can only use the minimum amount of force required to end the conflict and bring peace. We momentarily suspend human rights in a quest ultimately to preserve them. Jack Bauer (along with his writers and most viewers) sees himself engaged in a "war on terror." When Jack is in a gunfight with terrorists and he shoots to kill, it is clear, to him and to viewers, that he is in the midst of a war. But when Jack moves to torture someone who has been restrained, and sometimes may be an innocent, the lines are not always so clear. It is important to look at what Jack has said in these moments of confrontation.

One of the most revealing encounters came in season two. After an extensive chase and difficult capture, Jack Bauer interrogated terrorist Syed Ali, seeking information about the nuclear bomb hidden in Los Angeles. Bauer asked Ali several times to reveal the location of the hidden nuclear bomb. When Ali refused, Bauer had a monitor brought into the room so that Ali could see that CTU had kidnapped his wife and two sons. When Ali still would not talk, Bauer leaned in close and said, "I despise you for making me do this" (2-12). Then Bauer ordered the agents to kill Ali's eldest son. In his grief, Ali relented and gave the location of the bomb. As agents carried Ali away, Kate Warner in horror accused Jack of being "just like them." Moments later, though, she observed on the screen that the son was still alive, and with relief she realized that Jack's actions were an elaborate bluff.

This scene is classic 24. In this moment we feel Jack's dilemma. He needs to find the bomb to save millions of lives; he must find a way to get Ali to talk. Violence is the language that terrorists use. We are left with the question, must our hero also engage in violence? If he does, is he "just like them"? How do we distinguish "good guys" from "bad guys" in the world of 24? How does Jack distinguish himself from those he confronts?

Jack believes his actions directly follow from Ali's; he believes that he has no choice. In this case, we saw Jack using a bluff, but we know from other episodes that there are times when he feels he has to go the next step and actually use the violence he threatens. How does he go about making these decisions? Since he believes that he is in a war, started by someone else, Jack feels he is justified in not going through normal channels to combat the larger threat. He ignores the need for warrants, helps suspects break out of jail, holds people hostage, pretends to rob a convenience store, and kidnaps and tortures suspects. Many people around him, notably those sticklers from Division, balk at his tactics, but Jack says that he is willing to face the consequences as long as he can say that he stopped Victor Drazen, Syed Ali, Habib Marwan, and others. He believes that it is necessary to break the laws he wishes to uphold for the sake of the greater good. Terrorists do not follow the rules, and if he is to be successful in stopping them, then he too must not be constrained. In season three, Jack was willing to push the terrorist's daughter into a building with a lethal virus. Jack is fully willing to exploit the terrorists' connections to family, as they have with him. But Jack would argue that there are limits to his actions—that his actions are primarily defensive, that they are reactions to the terrorists' previous actions. If he is to protect the lives of hundreds of thousands of noncombatants, then he must resort to extreme tactics. He feels that he has no choice; he despises the terrorists for forcing his hand. Jack, as a utilitarian martyr, steps forward to engage in actions that are "necessary" in his worldview. And he sacrifices his own humanity in the process.

Season four's debate surrounding the interrogation of Joseph Prado is the most illuminating of 24's torture sequences (and there are many over the show's run), in showing how Jack thinks about his breaches of laws that are designed to preserve human rights, basic American values. Prado possessed information for locating the terrorist mastermind Habib Marwan. When CTU obtained Prado, Marwan called Amnesty Global and complicated matters for CTU. David Weiss, the representative from Amnesty Global, argued that the interrogation could not "play out in a back room with a rubber hose." Jack responded, "I hope you can live with that" (4-18). President Logan, though, would not authorize torture, even with Jack's arguments. Frustrated, Jack and Bill Buchanan hatched another plan: they would release Prado so that a rogue Jack Bauer could take matters into his own hands. Jack did indeed kidnap Prado in the parking lot and started an interrogation. Emphasizing from the start that he wanted Marwan and not Prado, Jack only started using torture when Prado did not cooperate. Jack broke fingers and placed a knife to Prado's throat before Prado finally talked. When the interrogation was over, Jack took Prado back to CTU for medical care. When Audrey put the pieces together and confronted Jack, he responded by saying, "What did you expect me to do?" He argued that his actions were absolutely necessary, that the immanent threat trumped normal procedures. Audrey countered that Jack could not operate "outside the line" and not expect consequences.

Jack, in a melancholic tone, said, "Trust me. No one understands the consequences better than me. No one" (4-19). Various characters responded in positive and negative ways to Jack's actions, but the debate withered in the threat of the pending detonation of a nuclear warhead in an undisclosed U.S. city. Jack went on to even greater questionable activity by season's end, invading the Chinese consulate to kidnap a Chinese citizen—an action that would haunt him in later seasons.

Using what we have learned from seasons two and four, we can conclude the following: Jack believes that he must do whatever is necessary to stop terrorist threats. Terrorists are attacking the United States, both what it stands for and the people who live there. Jack sees himself making sacrifices that will ultimately preserve America. Torture becomes one of those sacrifices. He does not want to hurt others; he always asks for their compliance and only resorts to a physical response when they resist. Many times Jack has not resorted to torture. When he finally captured Habib Marwan in season four, he felt that torture would be ineffectual in the short term and chose to negotiate with him. This is not an exception; Jack has negotiated with several other individuals along the way. Frequently, though, Jack has decided that torture was necessary during interrogation—that someone needed to be broken before they would reveal the necessary information. He himself has been the victim of torture—most notably in season two when he was literally tortured to death (but revived for further interrogation) and later when he was in China in the twenty months between seasons five and six.

He told Audrey that no one knows better than he does what the costs of his actions are. Helplessly he watched as Audrey drifted away from him because she could not handle being with him now that she had seen with her own eyes what his job required of him. Season three ended with Jack finally shedding tears after all he had been called to do during that day, and season six ended with Jack apparently sacrificing his relationship with Audrey because he loved her and did not want to pull her into his violent world. Jack knows the cost.

IS THERE NO OTHER CHOICE?

Season six ended with Jack in a crisis of faith. In the last minutes of this twenty-four-hour period, Jack broke into Senator Heller's home and, while holding a gun to the senator, yelled his discontent, saying that Heller had not tried hard enough to get him back from China. The leaders of the country that he had loved and protected had betrayed him by not going after him until it served their own interests (when they could trade him to a terrorist who was sponsoring suicide bombers on American soil). Jack believed that a sense of loyalty should have prompted them to try harder to obtain his release; he believed that he would not have abandoned Senator Heller in a similar situation (he had rescued Heller from terrorists at the beginning of season four). Senator Heller remained silent on this issue, choosing to focus more on Jack's concern for Audrey, arguing that Jack could not protect Audrey from the world of violence that he would always inhabit. Jack had tried to leave CTU three times before—after his wife's death, after being relieved of his job, and in an effort to avert a national crisis with the Chinese—but each time he had eventually returned to field work. Was Heller right? Jack demanded that the senator help him "get his life back," but then moments later sacrificed Audrey out of love, as if he had come to believe Heller's accusation. The season ended with Jack alone and a series of questions. We were left wondering where he would go now. Jack has reinvented himself numerous times but always maintained his apparent center of value, the United States. Now that he feels betrayed, what will organize his life? Who will he choose to be? Have the costs been too great?

How are we viewers to understand Jack Bauer in relation to his life of violence? In many ways it would be sanctimonious for us to judge his actions from a safe distance. We can admire Jack's heroism, his frequent sacrificing of his life and his dreams for others, while also mourning his losses. Yet we can also be, as he seems to be on numerous occasions, deeply troubled by his violence. Does he have any other choice? A number of people would say here that virtuous people will get "dirty hands" in politics; that there is no other way. A significant number of ethicists in America have argued for the limited use of violence in a just war. And if anyone embodies just-war theory, it is Jack Bauer. However, there are others, like H. Richard Niebuhr, who remind us that there is another way. Niebuhr, a Christian theologian, believed that forgiveness has transformative power. His thought shares similarities to that of Christian pacifists, like John Howard Yoder, Stanley Hauerwas, and John Milbank, who have argued that the politics of Jesus represent a true alternative to the violence in the world. Yoder sees Jesus' example calling Christians to a sacrificial pacifism that is geared toward reconciliation with others. What would Jack's life look like if he devoted as much energy and creativity toward diplomacy and humanitarian efforts, promoting peace, as he did toward CTU ops? H. Richard Niebuhr would remind us that such a move would bring a radical change in his values. Supporters of just war, most likely Jack Bauer included, are unlikely to be convinced; they would argue that too many lives would be lost in the process. Pacifists understand that, but argue that in the process our humanity, instead, would be lost. The long-running debate may never be settled in this world. It is a broken one, and many believe that violence can only be met with violence. Yet how great is the cost? Jack Bauer knows, and it haunts him.

———

BRETT CHANDLER PATTERSON teaches theology and ethics at Anderson University in South Carolina. He studied at Furman University, Duke University, and the University of Virginia. He has written several essays recently analyzing ethical themes in pop culture—responsibility in Spider-Man (published by BenBella), redemption in *Lost*, and the fight for social order in *Batman: No Man's Land*. He is currently working on a book analyzing the fantasies of C. S. Lewis, J. R. R. Tolkien, Orson Scott Card, and Gene Wolfe.

REFERENCES

Hauerwas, Stanley. *Peaceable Kingdom*. Notre Dame: University of Notre Dame Press, 1983.

Milbank, John. *Theology and Social Theory*. Cambridge, MA: Basil Blackwell, Inc., 1990.

Niebuhr, H. Richard. *Christ and Culture*. New York: Harper and Row, Pub., 1975 (1951).

_____. *Faith on Earth*. New Haven, CT: Yale University Press, 1989.

_____. *Meaning of Revelation*. New York: Collier Books, 1960 (1941).

_____. *Radical Monotheism and Western Culture*. Louisville, KY: Westminster/John Knox Press, 1970 (1960).

_____. *The Responsible Self*. New York: Harper & Row, Pub., 1963.

Yoder, John Howard. *The Politics of Jesus*. Grand Rapids, MI: William B. Eerdmans Pub. Co., 1992 (1972).

Honey Traps, Romeos, and Blackmail

Love, Sex, and Family in Espionage

PAUL LYTLE

1

In many ways, the first episode of *24* established the theme. When we first met Jack Bauer, he was not at work, poring over intelligence, or out in the field roughing up some terrorist, but at home with his family. His chief concern in that first episode was not the terrorists at all (even though we saw a great deal of the terrorists as they began their evil plot), but his daughter. Sure enough, Kim slipped out the window just as Jack was being called in to work; the conflict between country and family began within the first hour of this epic story.

It wasn't very long before we found out that Jack once had an affair with Nina Myers, one of his coworkers, though it was late in the season when we discovered that she had been working against CTU from the beginning. She had been using Jack's feelings and trust to obtain intelligence.

These individual plot lines are all eventually resolved. But while these particular problems are solved, sex, love, and family remain important themes throughout the series. The agents at CTU seem able to withstand all sorts of torture and coercion except when it comes to these three areas of life. In love, whatever form it may take, we see their Achilles' heel at last. And it is at that heel that the enemies strike.

2

And why should it not be this way on television? After all, real-life espionage is much the same way. 24 is not just trying to steam up the show a little when they have these elements involved in espionage. These personal parts of our lives have been exploited for intelligence from the beginning of time. And contrary to popular belief, most double agents are not spying against their own countries for money alone. There's normally something else involved, and quite often that "something else" has to do with sex, love, or family.

This is exactly why Jack's family keeps being drawn into the story, as well as the personal lives of the villains and other agents. These people value more in life than simply their jobs, and those other interests and pursuits can't help but get mixed up in their work.

3

Those other interests and pursuits are sometimes less than noble. In Martin Belkin's case, the personal pursuit responsible for his victimization was a very common weakness—sex.

In the first episode, we met Mandy. She was sitting next to Belkin, a photographer hired to take pictures of then-presidential candidate David Palmer, on a plane. Belkin was on his way to meet Palmer, so naturally, he had a pass that would allow him to gain access to the candidate, and Mandy (our first villain) wanted it. There are a number of ways she could have gone about it, but her method was perhaps the most direct. She had sex with him in the airplane bathroom and, while there, spirited away his pass.

4

This plot is not new. Sex and power have been intertwined since the dawn of time—as in the Book of Judges, in the story of Samson and Delilah. The Philistines, in search of a way to neutralize Samson's strength, go to Samson's wife Delilah and offer her 1,100 pieces of silver if she finds out where his strength lies. She fails three times; it isn't until she uses their relationship to manipulate him that she finds success. "How can you say, 'I love you,'" she asks him, "when your heart is not with me? You have deceived me these three times and have not told me where your great strength is" (2 Judges 16:15). It proves too much, and Samson confesses that if his hair were to be cut, he would lose his strength. Thanks to Delilah's betrayal, the Philistines are able to trap him at last.

In the *Iliad*, Hera also uses sex to advance her own cause, though in a slightly different way. According to the *Iliad*, even the gods took sides in the Trojan War; Zeus was helping the Trojans while Hera, his wife, aided the Greeks. Hera, knowing she could not counter Zeus's strength outright, removes him from the battle by seducing him. While they are occupied, the Greeks begin to take the upper hand.

A similar story appears in Texas legend: Sam Houston was able to catch Santa Anna off guard at the Battle of San Jacinto because a woman distracted the Mexican leader with sex while Houston charged. (This woman was the one who inspired the song "The Yellow Rose of Texas.")

These examples give us an idea of how sex was used for information, manipulation, and deception even millennia ago. The art of spying has not changed all that much since.

5

Victor Cherkashin was an officer in the KGB during the Cold War. He was a frequent contact for both Aldrich Ames and Robert Hanssen, two of the most infamous and destructive traitors to the United States in recent history. In his memoir, Cherkashin describes recruitment and blackmail techniques in detail.

Sometimes a blackmail opportunity would just fall into his lap. One British diplomat, who was married, would often have sex with prostitutes in his car. Of course Cherkashin was quick to act. "We . . . took photographs and confronted him with the evidence," he wrote (49). Easy enough.

Other attempts took a little more effort. Cherkashin would often send attractive operatives out as "swallows," which he defined as "male or female agents sent to seduce targets" (49).

Larissa was one of these agents. Her charm caused an employee of the British embassy, Edward Johnson, to fall in love with her. They made love in an apartment "stuffed . . . with eavesdropping bugs and hidden cameras" (50).

Cherkashin used the relationship to compromise Johnson further. Through her relationship with him, Larissa persuaded him to sell hard currency, an illegal act. Armed with the sale of the money and the moral crime of the affair, Cherkashin and Larissa made the attempt to blackmail Johnson. The mission failed. Johnson went to the embassy, told all, and was transferred out.

It's probably not so surprising that sex is used for the benefit of the state, but what is perhaps surprising is how casually it is used. In this case, the plan was a long shot to begin with, and yet Cherkashin doesn't seem to have any regrets about having Johnson seduced in this way, much less asking Larissa to participate for what promised to be very little, if any, gain.

Cherkashin explains why he was willing to do it: "I knew it was a necessary part of protecting the Motherland" (52). That is all the reason he needed. Without Larissa's testimony, we can only assume that her motives were similar.

It wasn't just the Soviets. France used the same technique as recently as the 1990s "to break the alleged American economic espionage effort" against them (Hitz 99). Supposedly, an American woman was working undercover in France to steal technology. While she was using her lover for connections, she did not know that this lover, a spy working for France, was reporting all of her moves to his superiors.

6

Mandy's actions in the first episode may have surprised us, even shocked us. But while those actions were undoubtedly good for ratings, Mandy was playing out the realistic role of the "swallow."

In Mandy's case, her goal was to obtain something physical. She was not really interested in putting Belkin in a compromising situation and blackmailing him (after all, he would be dead soon, since Mandy planned to blow up the plane and parachute to safety). But it's not

46

always information the spy needs. In this case, it was a pass to get near Palmer. In Larissa's case, sex was a tool to gain trust. After all, sex was not a crime, and Cherkashin was looking for a crime. But the trust she gained via sex gave them the opportunity to set up a crime.

7

In another instance in 24, sex was just a way to buy time.

In season five, the first lady, Martha Logan, discovered in bits and pieces that her husband, President Logan, was committing treason. Bauer was on President Logan's tail, and needed to get to the presidential retreat before Logan left it—but was too far away to make it in time. So he contacted Martha.

Martha, in turn, played the "swallow" for a little while. She seduced her husband and delayed him long enough for Jack to get there.

Though Martha Logan was not a trained spy and was not employed in espionage, she definitely played the part here. Her actions were different than Larissa's in that President Logan was her lawful husband, but she was still involved in sex for the benefit of the country rather than love, lust, or recreation, just as Larissa was.

8

Why does it work? Why, if you knew you were in a position where the smallest liaison could compromise your country, would you risk it? Why, for that matter, risk so much for *any* sort of payoff, financial, sexual, or otherwise?

It should not seem so foreign to us. Our own politicians risk their careers quite often for a sexual liaison or other payoff. From Bill Clinton to Newt Gingrich, we've had several of these scandals in even the last generation.

Cherkashin explains why he was able to recruit or trick other spies:

> Spies tend to focus on their personal problems, not political
> ones. Most don't want to betray their countries and refuse to
> think of themselves as traitors. They simply want to solve an
> immediate problem or satisfy a kindled ambition, and spying
> offers itself as a possibility. (115)

Perhaps, ultimately, we can say the same thing about photographers, presidents, and embassy employees. When confronted with a personal problem or desire, it is often difficult to concentrate on the political ramifications, especially when you are not expecting them. Few people, even those in political careers, would think that a girlfriend or boyfriend is hanging around simply for some inside information. Even if they thought about it when picking someone up at a bar, the natural assumption is that there would be very little information a person could get in one night, even if that person were looking for it. Meanwhile, the promise of sex or love or companionship is a tempting and powerful one.

In the end, when it comes to lust, desire, or loneliness, few are terribly worried about how they might be compromised.

9

There's another approach, one that is longer-term and riskier but seems to be successful in providing a reliable and continual source of information. In this case, instead of setting up a torrid and embarrassing liaison that can be used for blackmail purposes, the spy establishes a serious and loving relationship with the target, and uses the target's connections and trust to infiltrate his or her organization.

Blackmail and sex often produce unreliable results. If you are trying to use them to force information from someone, it is very likely that the answers to your questions will be incomplete or false. Sex does not create the sort of bond where the target will willingly betray his country. Blackmail creates hostility and mistrust. Sometimes it works very well, but its effects are limited, and usually only temporary.

It is better that the target not even know that he is giving up the information. That is tough to accomplish with sex and impossible with blackmail, but it is possible with love. Willing defections (someone who is willing to sell out his country for a price) might be preferable, but using love can actually create a target that willingly helps without knowing that he is helping.

The agents sent for this purpose are called "Romeos."

10

Markus Wolf, a Communist spymaster in East Germany during the Cold War, preferred this method of spying and used it often. He targeted then-West German Chancellor Konrad Adenauer, and sent an agent code-named "Felix" to infiltrate the organization.

Felix was the first "Romeo" used by Wolf. He began to hang out with the employees of the Chancellor's office until he met a secretary code-named "Norma." Once their relationship began, things happened naturally:

> Felix was invited to meet [Norma's] colleagues for bowling or office excursions on the Rhine pleasure boats. Turning on his southern charm, he could be the life and soul of the party, telling jokes, dancing with the women, and drinking heartily with the men. (Wolf 126)

Felix could not risk marriage, as it would involve a background check, but he and Norma did move in together and lived that way for years. All the while, Felix was using their relationship to get information. As a trusted friend of Norma's coworkers, many doors were opened to him.

Wolf eventually got word that the West German government was on to Felix, and hurriedly pulled Felix out. Norma may never have known the real reason he left.

11

The intelligence benefits of this arrangement are obvious, but the risk is very great. Obviously, the longer a spy is in the same place, the better chance of him being discovered. Many of these "Romeos" have to be extracted.

The other danger is that a spy who romances a target for years will often (very naturally) develop feelings for that target. Felix returned to East Germany "in a terrible state" (Wolf 126). In playing a game with love, he had fallen in love as well.

Despite these dangers, Wolf actively used "Romeos" until 1979.

12

We have seen a couple of long-term "Romeos" in *24*. The first was Nina herself. Her relationship with Jack put CTU in more danger, probably, than the rest of the plot combined. The intelligence she gathered kept CTU one step behind throughout the day, and compromised CTU's security on subsequent days as well.

The implications of this are astounding. Her betrayal not only cost CTU valuable time and effort (as well as lives), but also cast doubt on the whole organization. Who, then, *could* they trust? When trying to stop a terrorist plot while seriously pressed for time, such doubts and second-guessing can only make the team less effective.

Nina was probably more successful as a "Romeo" than Felix was. Not only was she connected because of her relationship with Jack, but she also worked inside CTU. Obviously, she had defected at some point and become a double agent, so she was not purely (or not only) a "Romeo," but she did use the same techniques.

Nina differed from Felix in that she didn't seem to have been in danger of falling in love with her target. Especially in her subsequent appearances, she was remarkably cold, and in light of those later appearances, it is hard to believe that she ever loved Jack, or that it was ever more than a job to her. She might have been the perfect double agent— disloyal, ambitious, greedy, cold, and knowledgeable. The interweaving of both the traditional double agent role with the "Romeo" approach ensured that she would be perfectly placed when she was needed.

13

Perhaps a better example of a "Romeo" was Theo Stoller from the fifth season. Intelligence-selling mercenary Collette Stenger was such an important target for Germany that they sent an intelligence agent, Stoller, on a long-term mission to find evidence against her. Part of that mission was to become her lover. While he was getting closer, Stenger was being remarkably guarded about her business, and that forced Stoller's mission to continue over a very long period of time.

His path crossed Jack's when CTU was trying to find Stenger for different reasons, and the conversation between the two was revealing.

Stoller talked about wanting to bring the woman in, but at the same time about how it was impossible to spend that much time with someone and not have feelings for her. He was sorry to let it end.

But he does let it end, and he gives up Stenger for something even more valuable to his country. For a "Romeo" to be successful, the state must come first. These agents must get close to someone and then betray that person's trust. It's not simply that Stoller betrayed Stenger at the end; he was betraying her with every step.

14

The game of espionage does not always involve such complicated and long-term methods. Sometimes the simple and quick approach works the best, which is perhaps why "swallows" have been employed for so long. With that in mind, the use of a target's family members should not surprise us. In 24, where time is definitely of the essence, this particularly disconcerting form of blackmail has been useful to both CTU and the terrorists.

Does it happen in the real world of espionage? It does. We may be more used to hearing of such threats in mafia movies or perhaps news stories about South American drug dealers, but in the Cold War such tactics were utilized as well.

15

Cherkashin relates one such episode: America had a diplomat at the U.N., a Ukrainian named Constantine Warwariv, whom Russia suspected of being a former Nazi collaborator. If it could be proved, the information could be used as propaganda against the United States.

Cherkashin's talk with Warwariv was not going terribly well when Cherkashin tried to change tactics. He said, "It's unfortunate you're being so uncooperative. We also have unofficial levers at our disposal. Don't forget your sister still lives on Soviet territory" (126).

In this particular case, Cherkashin's intelligence was old. The sister had already immigrated to America. It does, however, illustrate how far a spy will go for a little information.

16

Jack is definitely guilty of this sort of action. In the second season, he interrogated a terrorist named Syed Ali who was more than willing to die for his cause, and Jack, unsurprisingly, was getting nowhere.

And so Jack went after something more important to Ali than his own safety. He had Ali's two sons tied up. And then he threatened their lives.

When Ali continued to stonewall, Jack ordered the older son to be shot. After witnessing the event, Ali cracked.

Jack was bluffing in that case. The death was faked, and we saw almost immediately that Ali's son was okay. The technique remained the same whether the boy died or not, however. An innocent bystander was still brought into the situation to force someone's hand.

17

In season five, Jack went a little further than a mere bluff. After successfully tracking down former CTU employee Christopher Henderson with his wife Miriam at their home, Jack was making no headway in his attempts to question him; Henderson knew all the tricks already, and he would not break. Jack threatened to shoot him, but Henderson didn't care.

So Jack shot Miriam in the leg.

Henderson still didn't crack, though—which, again, is the danger of blackmail. It doesn't always work for either CTU or the terrorists.

18

It doesn't take a great leap of logic to see how family can be a liability for a spy. After all, we've seen enough movies where the family of the hero has been threatened in an attempt to keep the hero from saving the day.

In the first season, we saw that very strategy used, unsuccessfully, on Jack. Teri and Kim, Jack's wife and daughter, were kidnapped to force Jack into killing David Palmer. Jack pretended to go along with Kim and Teri's captors while still working for the good guys. Appearing to do so gave him some time to strike back, and he was able to save them both (though Teri was killed later) while still protecting Palmer and saving the day.

19

In season three, Tony Almeda was put into a similar situation. When his wife, Michelle, was captured by Saunders, Tony was forced to help him so that she would not be killed. Tony helped more actively than Jack had, even going so far as to release Saunders's wife in order to try to make a trade. Jack caught him in time, though, and together the two of them were able to turn the situation against the terrorists.

20

Family is often used *against* an agent, but sometimes it can be used *by* an agent, as a resource. In the second season, we were introduced to Marie Warner. While the audience (and certain characters) suspected her fiancé of being a villain in the early episodes, it was eventually revealed that Marie herself was the bad guy: she was a member of Second Wave, a terrorist organization.

She was able to quite effectively use her family's love and connections for her own ends. In the beginning, she had been using her father's business to funnel money into Second Wave. As the story continued, she increasingly took advantage of her family's connections and love, and her family suffered for it. After her fiancé discovered the truth, for example, he could not help but wonder out loud whether the engagement had not all been a sham. He seemed to still be wondering it when Marie shot him.

21

For Marie Warner, her family was a resource. But can a family be a real asset? Not merely a tool to be used, but a source of support and even material assistance? Certainly families can provide spies the emotional support they need. But many times, they can do even more. In the early part of the twentieth century, in fact, families played a vital role in Britain's intelligence community.

Tammy M. Proctor explores this issue in detail in her article "Family Ties in the Making of Modern Intelligence." Leading up to and during World War I, Britain was very careful to create networks of families within its intelligence world. Sometimes this was accomplished as simply as hiring the daughter of an agent to work as a secretary. Sometimes, a whole family would be placed in a hostile country to spy. The reason was simple: "Families were tight-knit groups with deep ties of loyalty and affection who managed to keep their activities quiet and 'in the family'" (Proctor 457).

In other words, a new spy in a hostile place would instantly and automatically have a much higher level of loyalty and motivation if she had a family member on the same mission. She would be less susceptible to bribes, blackmail, etc., simply because to betray her country would also mean betraying her husband or brother or mother. They were "more reliable and loyal since more than their own lives were at stake" (Proctor 452).

Would Aldrich Ames have turned in so many undercover CIA agents had one of his family been on the list? We cannot say for sure, but we can certainly assume that most agents would hesitate to defect if it would result in the imprisonment or death of a family member. Acquaintances and strangers are easier to betray.

22

In 24's third season, we discovered that Kim was working at CTU. This was quite a shock (at least it was for me), since we had grown to expect a certain immaturity and childishness from Kim. Besides, she had never before shown any sort of aptitude with intelligence, and suddenly she was working as an analyst! I found the move a little hard to believe.

My suspicion was that the producers were trying to keep her in the show, but couldn't think of another way to do it. For all I know, that actually was the real reason behind it. But the move also makes a certain amount of sense—for Jack, and for CTU.

In the first two seasons, we had discovered several double agents working within CTU. Quite frankly, Jack couldn't trust anyone. Considering how often he steps outside the law and protocol to get something done, he needed someone inside CTU that could help him. In later seasons, that person would be Chloe, but Chloe had not proven herself yet.

In season three, it was Kim.

It is interesting to note that Jack did not trust Kim enough to bring her into his complete plan, but when he was in a bind, he called her.

Kim is naturally more loyal to her father than to either CTU or the government. She may have questioned his orders, but she was less apt to do so than anyone else in the building. She conceded to his wishes more quickly and more fully than a normal CTU agent would do.

As far as her presence at CTU, *that* was her real value to Jack.

Of course, her presence also had a value to CTU. Jack had already proven that he was very willing to disobey orders or go against CTU to do what he thought was right. Kim's presence at CTU tied Jack more closely to the organization and, in theory, gave them leverage to keep him in line. Her skill on the computer may very well have been secondary.

23

It is no accident that the only things that really get to Jack, the only things that even come close to breaking him, come in the forms of love and family. Kim is a soft spot for Jack, as is Audrey Raines, his romantic interest in the later seasons. Even so, long after the events of the first season, Jack is still affected by the death of his wife. Here is a man who has literally been killed and brought back to life, tortured, kidnapped, and taken to China for more torture, and it is love that causes him to question his purpose.

In the final episode of the sixth season, Jack voiced his longing to leave counterterrorism. He had longed for this before, and had left CTU several times because of it. Audrey's father, James Heller, echoed what Jack himself must have secretly been afraid of: that he could never escape it, and that it would only destroy Audrey like it destroyed Jack's wife.

Six seasons have proven Heller right on this. Jack cannot escape the life he's chosen—but love still binds him, keeping him wanting something more than what he can safely have.

24

The real-life stories of sex, love, and family discussed here rarely have happy endings. Even if the mission were accomplished, many of the participants left with less ability to trust, with some amount of hurt and anger, or with real heartbreak. We have seen enough of Jack to realize that is almost impossible to avoid. We recognize the truth in Heller's words, and we know that Audrey will pay the price for Jack's commitment to his job and country; she's already paid it several times over. We know that Jack's relationship with Kim will never really be healed as long as he is at CTU.

Perhaps Tammy M. Proctor can give us some hope for Jack. Perhaps in doing the job together with family and loved ones, Jack can keep both parts of his life intact. After all, he was closest to Kim during season three, when she was working at CTU.

The way these relationships have been going, however, that does not seem likely. And neither does it seem likely that Jack will ever really succeed in leaving counterterrorism behind. Every attempt to do so has failed. In the end, it is most likely that Jack will save the world a few more times, but in doing so destroy his own life completely.

PAUL LYTLE is an author and musician living on the southwest side of Houston, Texas. He earned a Bachelor of Arts from Houston Baptist University in English and political science with a specialization in creative writing, and will soon earn a Master of Liberal Arts degree. His primary skill seems to be gathering comic books and gently used paperbacks and hoarding them. This is his third contribution to the Smart Pop series, the other two being in *The Man from Krypton* and *Webslinger*. He hopes that there will be many more in the future, especially if they give him an excuse to buy more DVDs. More of his writings, as well as news and other projects, can be found at www.paullytle.com.

REFERENCES

Cherkashin, Victor, with Gregory Feifer. *Spy Handler*. New York: Basic Books, 2005.

Hitz, Frederick P. *The Great Game: The Myth and Reality of Espionage*. New York: Knopf, 2004.

Proctor, Tammy M. "Family Ties in the Making of Modern Intelligence." *Journal of Social History* 39.2 (Winter 2005).

Wolf, Markus, with Anne McElvoy. *Man Without a Face: The Autobiography of Communism's Greatest Spymaster*. New York: Random House, 1997.

Hacking Jack Bauer

JIM RAPOZA

Wwhile 24 has many themes, the one thing that is always at the core of the show is security. Whether it's the security of a presidential candidate, the city of Los Angeles, or the entire country, the main plot of every season of 24 hinges on one group of people trying to break down security measures (in order to cause harm) and another group dedicated to maintaining that security (in order to stop them). The people involved in these situations can be described in many ways: good guys, bad guys, police, terrorists, criminals, special agents. But there's another word that can be used to describe them all: hackers.

Mention the word "hacker "and most people think of some computer wiz who uses their elite (or l33t, as the hacker kids like to say) skills to break into corporate or government networks and steal sensitive information.

However, say "hacker" to programmers, security analysts, and other technology workers and they don't immediately think of criminals. In technology, hacker is often a term of respect, given to someone who knows how everything works (and who, if he doesn't know how something works, is willing to take the thing apart to figure it out). Good hackers are known for their ability to find creative solutions to almost any problem, whether it's circumventing a security barrier, pushing a computer beyond its normal capabilities, or using a tool for a purpose completely different from what it was intended for.

In the world of 24, the character who appears to best fit the hacker mold (really, using either definition) is Chloe O'Brien. Chloe is the show's übercomputer-geek/wiz. Throughout the years Chloe has used her l33t hacking *skillz* to defeat high-powered encryption, find data on destroyed cell phones and PDAs, repurpose satellites, and even access and control government networks (once comically doing so from a hotel bar while being hit on by a drunk).

Clearly, if you're looking for a hacker on 24, then Chloe is the obvious choice. But she isn't the only one. And I'm not referring to minor characters like Edgar or Morris.

No, there is one other character in 24 who fits all of the core definitions of a hacker, with demonstrated ability to circumvent security barriers, push things beyond their limits, and use tools for unique purposes.

That character is, of course, Jack Bauer himself.

While Jack does seem to be a capable user of technology, his skills are hardly advanced (though, like many other people, I would love to get a hold of one his cell phones, which seem to have more power and capability then any full-fledged personal computer I've ever used).

No, Jack Bauer is a hacker because of his ability to hack the real world.

In 24, Jack has displayed pretty much all of the characteristics of a hacker. Rather than doing so on computers and the Internet, Jack hacks real people and real-world situations. And of course, Jack has more than once brought a different kind of hacking into play, such as the time he cut off a mob snitch's head in order to get inside a criminal group.

To further prove my point, let's break down some of the core characteristics of the hacker and see if Jack Bauer has displayed them over the course of the six seasons of 24.

HACKERS PREFER DOING OVER SUPERVISING

If you don't get your hands dirty, either figuratively (by programming) or literally (by taking things apart), then you most likely aren't a true hacker. Unlike professors or executives, a hacker doesn't want to theorize about a potential technique or security crack. Hackers actually dig down and do it themselves. This is also the reason why true hackers never really graduate to management positions. If they aren't actively hacking, then they aren't happy.

Now let's look at Bauer. At the beginning of the first season of *24*, Jack held the position of Director at CTU in Los Angeles. But very quickly (for a variety of reasons including the kidnapping of his family) he ended up back in the field, in his true element.

This theme played out through the other seasons of *24*. Jack didn't last long as security advisor to the Secretary of Defense, nor did he succeed in his attempts to remain in hiding as a rig worker.

When watching a virtuoso hacker at work, you notice that they possess an almost cool, zen-like detachment as they go about their business. You think to yourself, "This person really knows what they're doing." When Jack is in the field, we are treated to the same type of detached coolness. It's no surprise that the other true hacker in the show, Chloe, is the one who most clearly recognizes Jack's skills. As Chloe said in an attempt to soothe the fears of a young man who doubted Jack's ability to plan their escape from a building surrounded by agents looking to arrest them in season five: "Relax, he's really good at this" (5-1).

A STANDARD HACKING TOOLKIT

Every hacker has a standard set of tools. For example, a network security hacker will start out with network-sniffing tools to look for any open ports and applications that can be exploited. If he finds something, he'll bring out some trusted scripts that have worked for him in the past in order to break through the weak points he has found. Also, hackers often have a style that characterizes them. Some value subterfuge, secrecy, and the ability to pass through systems unseen. Others rely on pure brute force techniques, breaking through barriers as quickly as possible to get what they need, regardless of any subsequent repercussions.

Jack Bauer's style definitely fits in the brute-force category.

Let's walk through a typical Jack hacking session as he employs his standard toolkit in order to liberate necessary information from a secured system (or in layman's terms, get a bad guy to tell him where the bombs are). Step one: Put gun to bad guy's head and yell directly in his face. Step two: Smack the bad guy around and threaten him (Jack has lots of good threat quotes, such as, "If you don't tell me what I want to know, then it'll just be a question of how much you want it to hurt"). Step three: It's finger-breaking time! Step four: Serious, actual, painful measures (remember, he's a brute force type of guy).

Sure, it's a brutal process, but like any good hacker, he falls back on things that work. And if you think comparing tortured people to hacked computer systems is a bit extreme, you should talk to some of the companies that have had their systems targeted by one of the Eastern European cyber-crime syndicates. They face pretty much all of the same steps, including threats (nice Web site you have there, be a shame if something happened to it), finger-breaking (typically in the form of denial of service attacks), and serious torture (polluted system registries and nasty rootkits). (No wonder so many of these sites pay ransom rather than face cyber-pain.)

USING TOOLS FOR PURPOSES OUTSIDE THEIR ORIGINAL DESIGN INTENT

The vast majority of the tools that hackers use weren't meant for hacking. For the most part they were designed to handle some mundane task but were adapted by hackers for use in other, more original ways. Most of the network-scanning tools that hackers employ were designed to help network administrators monitor and manage networks. Some software code hacking tools are good old-fashioned software development tools. Even some of the nastier security-hacking programs were originally designed to help companies find and secure potential problems in their systems.

In the world of 24, Jack Bauer has shown remarkable innovation when it comes to using common household and business items to solve a problem or circumvent a barrier. (Adding to the believability is that Jack never crosses over into the absurd MacGyver-type territory.)

So what are some good examples of ways Jack has used common items to hack the real world? He's used a plastic bag over the bad guy's head to potentially suffocate him. He's tied people up with pretty much any cord-like item at hand, and he once pulled the electrical cords from a lamp in order to torture a suspect (also his girlfriend's ex-husband) with electrical shocks.

Basically, if there's something lying around that Jack can use to either secure or hurt someone, then there's a good chance he will use it.

WILLINGNESS TO SACRIFICE IN ORDER TO ACHIEVE A GOAL

When hackers take on systems with strong security measures (either as a security consultant testing a company's defenses or as an actual bad guy trying to steal data), they face a wide array of defenses. One defense is known as a "honey pot." The general idea of a honey pot is that it looks like a real security hole that the hacker can use to get through system defenses when in truth it's a trap, designed to steer the hacker into a dead end where he can be stopped and even identified.

One way to defeat these types of security measures is for hackers to intentionally sacrifice one of their own resources in order to identify traps like honey pots, so that they will then be able to circumvent them using another, more effective hacking system. Sure, the hacker will lose a useful resource (probably in the form of a remote bot or zombie system that he took over previously), but he will be one step closer to his ultimate goal.

When it comes to sacrificing for his ultimate goal, Jack rarely hesitates. In fact, if there's anything worse than being one of Jack's enemies, it might be being his friends or coworkers. They are as likely to get shot by Jack as by a terrorist.

Jack once executed one of his successors as head of CTU in order to gain time to defeat the bad guys he was chasing. In one situation, Agent Michelle Dessler was captured by bad guys, able to achieve her own escape, and then sent back to the bad guys by Jack in order to make it easier for him to catch them.

When you think about it, the only time Jack went against the philosophy of sacrificing a colleague in order to gain time to beat the bad guys was in the first season, when he provided Nina Meyers with a bulletproof jacket in order to shoot her without killing her. Given how that worked out for him, it's no wonder he's become more ruthless when it comes to taking out a friend in order to reach his final goals.

HACKING UNDER COVER

While people tend to think of hackers in solely technical terms, many of the best hackers (especially among black hats) bring a strong social[1] element to their quests to defeat company security systems. Why bother gaining access to a company network when a simple call posing as an IT guy can convince an actual office worker to give up a user name and

---

[1] Social hacking, also known as social engineering, refers to tactics and strategies used to trick businesses, workers, and users into giving vital information and security access such as passwords to systems. Several technology security institutions offer courses in understanding social hacking.

password? And a simple walk through an office while dressed like a copier repair man can often yield hacking gold in the form of user names and passwords on Post-It notes attached to monitors. I even once heard of a case where a researcher testing a company's security processes found a piece of paper attached to a server room door that listed all of the most important user names and passwords for the company systems.

And when you think of it, this "disguise" type of hacking fits in well with traditional Hollywood and other fictionalized portrayals of people working in the spy business. The word "spy" itself is often interpreted as someone who can easily disguise themselves to fit into any situation.

But Jack Bauer isn't a normal spy, and the social hack does not seem to be one of his strong points. Like I pointed out earlier, he's a brute force kind of guy, and sneaking into someplace wearing a disguise is more the secretive, hidden hacker's M.O. Jack is much more likely to go into a place by kicking the door down, guns blazing.

But that doesn't mean Jack has never played the subterfuge card. He has entered a danger zone under the guise of a potential business client, another office disguised as a computing consultant, and even a high-rise while posing as a maintenance man. Probably his most extensive undercover job occurred between seasons, when he went undercover with a drug cartel—which you could call a success, except for how he ended up addicted to heroin.

This is definitely the weakest of Jack's hacking skills. Whenever he is supposedly undercover, he still looks pretty much just like Jack Bauer. I know if I worked in one of these offices that he entered covertly, I would be thinking, "Why does that contractor look like he wants to kill someone?"

KNOWING WHEN TO CALL FOR HELP

Very few hackers are good at everything. And good hackers recognize when some barrier or security measure is beyond their own ability to defeat. This is the point when many hackers look for help.

Perhaps you're a hacker who is highly skilled at network and software hacking, but you run into something using strong encryption that you can't handle yourself. If you're smart you have a trusted ally that you can turn to, who has the skills you don't. These types of allies are invaluable for helping you get around obstacles you wouldn't otherwise be able to defeat.

Jack's best hacker ally is Chloe. Whenever Jack needs someone tracked by satellite or evidence pulled from a destroyed computer, he relies on Chloe's considerable skills.

But there is another ally that Jack often turns to when a barrier seems insurmountable.

I am, of course, talking about the mysterious Agent Richards. Whenever there's a suspect that Jack can't crack, out comes Richards with his apparently horrific collection of pain-inducing materials. If there's any possibility of the suspect talking, Richards will get the information, and then Jack can get back to the hitting, running, shooting, and, of course, hacking.

SPEED

One characteristic of the best hackers, and especially the best code hackers, is speed. While the classic movie and TV portrayals of coders clicking away full speed on a keyboard are a bit exaggerated, they aren't that far off. Many code hackers work at a pretty blistering speed. Even beyond their pure typing skills, the best hackers have the ability to carry out an entire hacking exploit in very short order. At security and hacking conventions such as Black Hat, there are often contests to see who can defeat the security of some system or application in the shortest amount of time.

And come on, we're talking Jack Bauer here! What's the name of the show again? That's right, 24, as in one freakin' day! This is by far Jack Bauer's core hacking characteristic: he hacks at high speed. The clock is always ticking.

Does anyone else work at anything close to the same speed when it comes to this form of elite counterterrorism hacking? Of course not. If there was a competition to see who could stop a group of terrorists in the shortest amount of time, between Jack Bauer, James Bond, Jason Bourne, and Ethan Hunt, I would put my money on Jack.

In 24, Jack Bauer is skilled as a soldier, an officer of the peace, an espionage agent, and yes, as a brutal torturer. But it's the ways that he combines his skills that make him successful.

Like any true hacker, Jack Bauer doesn't see any problem as an end point. When a barrier comes up between Jack and his mission, he uses all the skills and information at his disposal to figure out a way to circumvent that problem.

Or, to put it in classic hacker speak: Jack is a *l33t h4x0r* and *l4m3rs* should *ph33r* his *m4d sk1llz.*

JIM RAPOZA was born and currently lives in Massachusetts. Over the years he has worked as a bike messenger, bar back, sports reporter, quality assurance engineer, and guitarist in punk rock bands. Since 1993 Jim has worked as a technology reviewer and analyst for high-tech magazines *PC Week* and *eWEEK.* Jim Rapoza's award-winning weekly column, "Tech Directions," delves into all areas of technology and the challenges of managing and deploying technology today.

Jack Bauer Is the Dirty Harry for the Age of Terrorism

LORIE BYRD

"Go ahead, make my day."

It is not hard to imagine Jack Bauer delivering "Dirty Harry" Callahan's famous line from the 1983 film *Sudden Impact*, or standing in for Callahan in the scene the line comes from, daring a man to go ahead and shoot the woman he's holding hostage at gunpoint so Callahan will have reason to fire.

Jack Bauer is, after all, the modern-day *Dirty Harry*—but instead of targeting armed robbers and serial killers, Bauer goes after terrorists intent on mass murder.

Not only are Dirty Harry and Jack Bauer similar characters, but they each won pop icon status in surprisingly similar times, Dirty Harry during a period of concern over increased violent crime and Bauer during the post–September 11 focus on the threat of terrorism.

Police Inspector Harry Callahan, portrayed by Clint Eastwood, rose to popularity in a series of five movies beginning with Dirty Harry in 1971 and continuing for seventeen years, through 1988's *The Dead Pool*. The Callahan character was loosely based on the chief investigator in the Zodiac Killer case, David Toschi, but Clint Eastwood made the character his own over the course of the series with his trademark squint, raspy voice, and deadpan delivery.

Dirty Harry was a new kind of fictional cop. In sharp contrast to the "just the facts, ma'am" officer epitomized by Jack Webb's Sergeant Joe Friday in the '50s and '60s, Callahan did not adhere to any procedural handbook. His high-action, in-your-face approach to detective work was a drastic departure from the daily routine police work depicted on shows like *Dragnet* and *Adam-12*.

Like *24*, the Dirty Harry movies thrive on an action-packed pace. Dirty Harry most often uses his unorthodox tactics when having to make split-second decisions in life-or-death situations, as when desperate criminals hold hostages at gunpoint. Jack Bauer is always working against the clock. (One of the lines most frequently used in parodies of the show is Jack's exhortation that, "There's no time." Another is, "I'm gonna need a hacksaw," but that is definitely another story.) After all, he only has twenty-four hours to save the world. His is the quintessential "ticking time bomb" scenario, in which extreme means are often necessary to beat the clock and save lives. This sense of urgency lets the audience allow their hero to engage in methods that might not otherwise seem acceptable—something that surely contributes to the popularity of both men.

Both Callahan and Bauer have problems with authority. Callahan is more openly contemptuous of his police chief and mayor, while Bauer is more deferential and respectful toward his CTU directors and the president, but both show little hesitation to disobey an order if they believe they know a better way to protect the public and put away the bad guys.

Most importantly, both characters tapped into the public's need to see a hero successfully responding to what was going on in the world at the time. Just as Harry Callahan embodied public frustrations over restrictions on law enforcement's ability to respond to rising violence in urban America beginning in the late '60s, Jack Bauer reflects the frustration of those who believe the government's ability to respond to terrorism is often hamstrung by legal technicalities and political constraints.

In desperate times (or even desperate-seeming times), there is always a market for the fearless hero in television and film. In *Dirty Harry*, the villain was a particularly vicious psychopath named Scorpio, based on the real-life Zodiac Killer who terrorized Northern California in the late

1960s. The movie's villain buried a young girl alive, but as horrible as that fictional scenario sounds, those living in the 1960s had already been traumatized by a number of shocking real-life murders, from the assassinations of presidents and civil rights leaders to the 1969 Tate-LaBianca murders committed by the Manson Family.

The villains of *24* are likewise drawn from real life. Today we live with the specters of Osama bin Laden, who killed some 3,000 Americans and others on September 11, and Abu Musab al-Zarqawi, who ordered the deaths of thousands of Iraqi women and children and is known to personally behead his enemies. Long after the images of 9/11 attacks left American television, new images of frightened hostages and beheaded journalists continued to appear.

In our world, villains are not always made to pay for their crimes. Both Osama bin Laden and the Zodiac Killer are still at large. One thing viewers can count on, though, is that Callahan and Bauer will not rest until they have caught, or killed, the bad guys.

In the late 1960s and '70s many Americans saw a world in turmoil. They saw the murder rate climb more than 400 percent from 1965 to 1985, and court decisions made it harder for police and prosecutors to win convictions. Traditional institutions seemed unable to adequately address the problems of urban crime and violence. These factors created an atmosphere in which the public was ready to root for a character like Dirty Harry, who was more concerned with the rights of law-abiding citizens to be free from violent crime than he was the rights of criminals.

Some significant Supreme Court decisions drove these changes transforming American society. In 1964, the U.S. Supreme Court, in a five-to-four decision, overturned the murder conviction of Danny Escobedo and recognized a suspect's right to an attorney during police interrogation in *Escobedo v. Illinois*. The court found that because Escobedo was not allowed an attorney, Escobedo's confession should not have been allowed as evidence in his trial. The Court subsequently defined the Escobedo Rule, which guarantees individuals the right to an attorney during police questioning. This made it much harder for the police to secure confessions.

In 1963, a man named Ernest Miranda was arrested for rape. He was aggressively interrogated by police and confessed to attempted rape and burglary. At trial, he was convicted and sentenced to twenty to thirty years. Miranda's lawyer appealed to the Arizona Supreme Court which affirmed the trial court's decision, emphasizing the fact that Miranda did not request legal counsel. The case was appealed to the United States Supreme Court, and on June 13, 1966, in *Miranda v. Arizona*, the Court ruled that due to the coercive nature of interrogation by police and the fact that he had not been made aware of his Fifth Amendment and other rights and had therefore not waived them, Miranda's confession should not have been allowed. His conviction was thereby overturned. One outcome of this decision, familiar to anyone who watches police dramas, was the Miranda Warning that now must be read to criminal suspects before they are questioned by police.

The public reaction to some of the changes resulting from these landmark cases granting specific, expanded rights to suspected criminals was reflected in the words of Harry Callahan in the following famous exchange:

> DISTRICT ATTORNEY ROTHKO: You're lucky I'm not indicting you for assault with intent to commit murder.
> HARRY CALLAHAN: What?
> DISTRICT ATTORNEY ROTHKO: Where the hell does it say that you've got a right to kick down doors, torture suspects, deny medical attention and legal counsel? Where have you been? Does Escobedo ring a bell? Miranda? I mean, you must have heard of the Fourth Amendment. What I'm saying is that man had rights.
> HARRY CALLAHAN: Well, I'm all broken up over that man's rights! (*Dirty Harry*)

Like Callahan, Bauer is not one to get "all broken up" over the rights of suspects he is interrogating or apprehending. And threats from either man are always to be taken seriously.

> HARRY CALLAHAN: (to suspect he has cornered) I know what you're thinking. *Did he fire six shots or only five?* Well, to tell you the truth, in all this excitement I kind of lost track myself. But being as this is a .44 Magnum, the most powerful handgun in the world, and would blow your head

clean off, you've got to ask yourself a question: Do I feel lucky? Well, do ya, punk? (*Dirty Harry*)

JACK BAUER: (to suspect he is questioning) You are gonna tell me what I want to know. It's just a question of how much you want it to hurt. (5-1)

HARRY CALLAHAN: Where's the girl?
THE KILLER: You tried to kill me!
HARRY CALLAHAN: If I tried to do that your head would be splattered all over this field. Now where's the girl? (*Dirty Harry*)

JACK BAUER: (to terrorist suspect) The only reason that you're conscious right now is because I don't want to carry you. (5-2)

Callahan and Bauer allow viewers the fantasy of hearing tough talk aimed at criminals without risking any of the real-world consequences that talk can sometimes entail.

It is understandable that a character like Jack Bauer would rise to prominence in response to the terrorist threat just as America had welcomed Dirty Harry to battle urban crime and violence thirty years earlier. Clint Eastwood said of Dirty Harry, "It's not about a man who stands for violence, it's about a man who can't understand society tolerating violence" (*The Dirtiest*).

The same could be said for Bauer, who does not engage in violence for the sake of violence, but rather engages in violence reluctantly in order to protect those unable to protect themselves. Frequently, he is the last line of defense between mass murderers and innocent, often unsuspecting, citizens.

The first season of *24* was set to air in the fall of 2001, but before it premiered America was attacked on September 11. Immediately, there was not only increased interest in the subject of terrorism, but also a desire to see the bad guys, the terrorists, pay. World developments in the years following the September 11 attacks only increased the American public's appetite for a hero who was more concerned about protecting innocent Americans than protecting suspected terrorists.

In the years following September 11, the intensity of the backlash from the abuses of detainees at the Abu Ghraib prison in Iraq and alleged abuses at the Guantanamo Bay detention facility in Cuba, as well as the government's reluctance to engage in profiling on the basis of race or nationality, led many to believe concerns for the civil rights of suspected terrorists was overshadowing the need to aggressively fight terrorism. The season five premiere of *24* was harshly criticized by some political conservatives for being overly sympathetic to ACLU positions by depicting an administration violating the civil liberties of Americans.

Yet also in that premiere, a plot depicting frustrated and paranoid suburban Americans taking out their frustrations on an innocent Muslim victim turned on a dime when the supposedly innocent victim was revealed to be a teenage terrorist ready to shoot dead the friend who had defended him during the attack.

While most television shows and movies were similarly reluctant to show Arabs or Muslims as terrorists, *24* was one place Americans could see terrorists portrayed as they most recently had appeared on their television newscasts, unlike in the 2002 motion picture based on the Tom Clancy book *The Sum of All Fears*. In the book, Muslim extremist terrorists acquire a thermonuclear device and decide to blow up the Super Bowl, hoping to ignite a nuclear war between the United States and Russia. In the year following the deadliest terrorist attack on America of all time, those making the movie version of the book decided it was best for the terrorists to be white supremacist Neo-Nazi types rather than Middle Eastern Muslim jihadists.

In its May 9, 2005, issue, *Newsweek* ran a story quoting a source who claimed military investigators had found evidence that American guards at Guantanamo Bay had engaged in extreme tactics to get terror suspects to talk, including at one point flushing a copy of the Koran down a toilet. (*Newsweek* failed to vet its sources: the U.S. Military–issued Koran is too big to fit down the toilet pipe and the toilets in the cells do not flush.) The story gained international attention. Two weeks following the original report, *Newsweek* retracted the Koran-flushing story, which had sparked violent riots in Afghanistan resulting in at least fifteen deaths, saying their source was mistaken. That same month, Amnesty

International harshly criticized the United States's detention center at Guantanamo Bay, calling the United States government guilty of "odious human rights violations" ("Cheney"). The United Nations later called for closing the facility.

In keeping with *24*'s willingness to insert real-world scenarios into their stories, the season five premiere showed the counterterrorism unit gaining valuable information about the number of nuclear bombs set to be detonated on U.S. soil from detainees at a Guantanamo Bay–style holding facility for those suspected of terrorist ties. Characters such as President Palmer's own sister spoke out against the detention facility and strong arguments were presented by characters on both sides of the issue, but ultimately the series showed valuable information being gained from some held at the facility. The real-life admiral in charge of the Guantanamo facilities makes the same claim.

Groups such as Amnesty International and the Council on American-Islamic Relations (CAIR) have fought for the rights of those suspected of terrorist activity. In November 2005, Amnesty International spoke strongly against Tony Blair's plans for new antiterror legislation and has at other times fought against proposals in other nations, including the United States, that would increase the powers of government officials to detain terror suspects.

In season four of *24*, one storyline captured not only the frustration of Americans who see some human rights advocates as more concerned with the rights of terrorists than those of law-abiding citizens, but also depicted a fantasy scenario where hero Jack Bauer worked around the rules to counter the efforts of just such a human rights group. In that episode, CTU apprehended an associate of a terrorist planning an attack with a nuclear device. The terrorist mastermind was worried that the associate would spill his guts under interrogation, but did not have anyone on the inside to quiet the guy. The terrorist called "Amnesty Global" (a fictional human rights watchdog group resembling Amnesty International) and told them that an innocent American citizen was being held by CTU without cause and was in danger of being handled roughly. A lawyer from Amnesty Global showed up at CTU with a court order prohibiting interrogation of the suspect without a lawyer present and putting many other restrictions on what the agents could do. The clock was ticking. The terrorists were in possession of a nuclear warhead and the codes to launch it, and the CTU agents couldn't do a thing about it. Bauer's answer to the problem was to ask CTU to release the suspect. He then resigned temporarily, becoming a private citizen. In the final scene of the episode, Bauer forced the terrorist into a vehicle at gunpoint and persuaded him (by breaking a few bones) to give up the needed information.

While fictional, this scenario—in which the civil rights group hampered the interrogation of a suspect who had valuable, life-saving information—in many ways fits the public perception of some groups advocating on behalf of suspected terrorists. Although many Americans might not have approved of Jack Bauer's solution in reality, it did give viewers a satisfying and successful resolution. Successful resolutions are something not guaranteed in the real world of counterterrorism.

Most people don't want their police officers acting outside of the law like Harry Callahan or torturing suspects as Jack Bauer sometimes does. The frustrations of a society battling the scourges of violent crime and terrorism are partly assuaged through the escapism Callahan and Bauer provide.

Americans have learned through their experiences with crime and terrorism that all the politicians and government officials in the world cannot keep them completely safe—especially considering the rules and laws which often constrain them. No wonder there is such a large audience for the ordinary individual who rises to extraordinary levels in reaction to dire circumstances, putting his own life at risk and sometimes breaking the rules to save others. They want to see happy resolutions to the problems they face, even if those resolutions are only on the flickering screen.

Dirty Harry's appeal eventually dimmed as police reforms in the early 1990s brought dramatic reductions in violent crime without sacrificing suspects' rights. As the social problem eased, Dirty Harry faded to black.

But the ever-present menace of terrorism shows no signs of abating—and Jack Bauer, the Dirty Harry for the age of terrorism, will likely be with us for a long time to come.

LORIE BYRD has been a big fan of television and a follower of politics her entire life. She graduated from N.C. State University in 1988 with a B.A. in political science. In April 2004, she became a contributor to Polipundit.com, a political blog, and in 2005 began writing at Townhall.com where she is currently a weekly columnist. She also writes a monthly column for the Washington, D.C., edition of *The Examiner* where she is a member of the Blog Board of Contributors. She now blogs at Wizbangblog.com and at LorieByrd.com. Lorie lives with her husband and two daughters in North Carolina.

REFERENCES

"Cheney Offended by Amnesty Criticism." CNN.com. 22 Aug. 2007.
  <http://www.cnn.com/2005/US/05/30/cheney.amnestyintl/index.html>
Dirty Harry, Dir. Don Seigel. Perf. Clint Eastwood. Warner Bros., 1971.
Escobedo v. Illinois, 378 U.S. 478 (1964).
Miranda v. Arizona, 384 U.S. 436 (1966).
The Dirtiest. 22 Aug. 2007. <http://www.the-dirtiest.com/dirty.htm>

Simulating Terror

Why Bush's Critics Love 24 *Even Though It Supports the Bush Doctrine*

AARON THOMAS NELSON

Why do *24* fans range from liberal to conservative? Since the show revolves around such pro-Bush issues as the War on Terror and the use of extreme measures to defeat terrorists, one might wonder why *24* garners fans from across the political spectrum.

The writers of the show are from mixed political backgrounds. Joel Surnow is a Republican who considers Rush Limbaugh a personal friend, while Howard Gordon is a self-described moderate Democrat (Heritage Foundation). But we must be careful in discussing this matter, since knowing someone is a "Republican" or a "Democrat" is not enough to understand his or her reason for supporting or protesting the War on Terror. Some of the Bush's biggest critics, after all, are his father's friends from his father's administration, as well as traditional conserva-tives (Reagan Republicans) who shun the notion of nation-building and interventionism (a notion George W. Bush himself shunned in his 2000 campaign.) The War on Terror is a decidedly "neoconservative" policy that breaks from sixty years of foreign policy steadily agreed upon by both parties. And yet, *24*, a show that supports the War on Terror, is still loved by those who criticize it.

The reason why the show is widely loved by many (ranging from Barbra Streisand to Judge Clarence Thomas) is because the show critiques Bush's War on Terror while at the *same time* lending credence to it. The critique lies in one of the most praised features of 24, the plot twist at the end of the season that reveals what was really going on in the previous episodes. Jihadists aren't really the ones behind the terror attack, as we initially thought. Someone else is—typically someone close to the president or close to CTU. The audience realizes, in the end, that CTU, or the president, or businessmen, are the cause of terror, not the Islamofascists. However, the show also conveys a world of ticking time bombs and absolute destruction if Jack Bauer does not act with moral exceptionalism—supporting the Bush Doctrine's own position on moral exceptionalism in the face of terror and rogue states, and giving credence to the War on Terror.

So, how do we reconcile the show's criticism and support of the Bush Doctrine while discussing 24's universal popularity? By realizing that the key to that popularity is not what "side" of the argument the show supports, but the fact that it raises the debate about the Bush Doctrine and the War on Terror to absolute importance.

THE BUSH DOCTRINE

Before examining how 24 supports and criticizes the Bush Doctrine, we should first examine what the Bush Doctrine is.

After 9/11, the Bush Administration rolled out a new foreign policy initiative that asserted the right to attack terrorists within the boundaries of sovereign nations, and to also attack those sovereign nations if the Administration believed it was harboring the terrorists ("Either you're with us or you're with the terrorists"). In essence, the doctrine empowered the Administration to "take the fight to the terrorists."

In his State of the Union address on September 20, 2001, President Bush explained that the attacks on September 11 were more than a breach of national security; they were an act of war committed by enemies of freedom whose "goal is remaking the world—and imposing its radical beliefs on people everywhere." Further, President Bush stated that al-Qaeda does not simply wish to destroy buildings and kill Americans, but "end a way of life." For Bush, after the day's attacks, "night fell on a different world, a world where freedom itself is under attack." The War on Terror was not only about national security, but about both the preservation of America's freedoms and "civilization." The very existence of our nation and our freedoms was at stake.

The Administration also included the right to wage pre-emptive wars in this new foreign policy initiative (The White House). The policy of pre-emption, though, was not necessarily born out of 9/11; rather, the policy was outlined a decade prior and first suggested by Paul Wolfowitz in 1992 while he was undersecretary of Defense for George H. W. Bush (who subsequently rejected it) (Tyler). It is precisely this element of pre-emption that is key to the Bush Doctrine. The Bush Doctrine depends on a claim that the United States is constantly under threat from terrorists and rogue states, and so cannot be morally judged in its acts of war, since it has the right to defend itself (White House 6, 13). This claim implies that any war the United States wages against these rogue states and terrorists is inherently just because their very existence threatens the security of the United States, and the war, therefore, is in self-defense. We no longer need to actually be attacked in order to claim the right of self-defense, nor do we need to detect a forthcoming attack, since terrorists can easily conceal themselves and deliver an attack covertly. We simply need to identify the *possibility* of a threat, which, for the Bush Doctrine, is already presumed to exist: al-Qaeda is constantly seeking to remake the world in accordance to its radical beliefs; concealed threats may exist anywhere and at any time. This moral exceptionalism built into the Bush Doctrine justifies both pre-emption and nation-building.

Finally, the Bush Administration stated that the War on Terror was a war against terrorist organizations that have a global reach, embrace an ideology of hate, and are enemies of freedom—al-Qaeda and al-Qaeda types. Their ideology specifically is a threat to the United States—it is the followers of this Salafi ideology that killed some 3,000 people on September 11, 2001—and therefore they are a rightful target.

How *24* Plays to the Critics of the Bush Doctrine

Critics of the Bush Doctrine usually describe it as unrealistic and damaging to the United States. Unilateralism in an age of globalization seems backward to critics; the idea that our actions under this doctrine would have no correlating reaction also seems implausible and thoughtless. Also, the doctrine comes off as a projection of U.S. power based on a simple (and fantastic) "us versus them" dichotomy. These sharp distinctions seem both risky and unnecessary to critics.

24 plays to these critics in three ways. First, the plot twist at the end of each season reveals that the cause of terrorism is something *other* than the terrorists who are engaging in terror. In season one, the terrorism turned out to be revenge against Jack Bauer and David Palmer for their actions taken in Kosovo two years prior. In season two, the terrorism was a ploy by Western businessmen in order to capitalize on a jump in oil prices. In season three, the mastermind behind the terrorism was actually Stephen Saunders, an MI-6 agent, who was a friend of Jack Bauer's and wanted to stop the American "war machine" (3-24). In season four, while Habib Marwan appeared to be the jihadist behind everything, in the final moments of the season it seemed that Westerners were again the true culprits—the season ended with Jack's brother picking up a phone to report Marwan's failed terrorist attack. And in season five, those same shady Westerners from season four, along with the president, were the ones behind the nerve gas terror. All of these surprise endings deliver the same message to the viewer: it is not the terrorists who are behind the terror, but rather us. We're the ones causing the terror. This effectively opposes the "us versus them" dichotomy the Bush Doctrine depends on.

Second, the plot twists also reveal that unintended consequences cannot be foreseen. Unilateralist pre-emptive strikes portrayed in the show lead to further conflict, something that seriously challenges the doctrine. In the first season, the terrorism is a response to Bauer's and Palmer's interventionist activities in Kosovo. And throughout the series, neither CTU nor Bauer detects the real cause of terror—those shady Western businessmen. They remain hidden, and their reactions to CTU and Jack Bauer's actions are unknown.

Also, the Bush Doctrine assumes that pre-emption and military intervention is a solution to terrorism. In 24 the terror does not end when that season's bad guys are killed. The true cause of the terror—those shady Westerners—successfully game CTU and the military, and remain undetected. As the show returns each season the conspiratorial revelations only get deeper (deeper even than the president). The very foundation of the Bush Doctrine is thrown into question as the television series continues—CTU believes it has defeated the source of the terrorism, when in fact it has not.

Third, our government's actions in the War on Terror are not portrayed as outside moral judgment. Politicians and policy makers are constantly revealed as complicit in the terrorism at the end of the season, be it the president, vice president, or CTU agents and officers. Having government insiders complicit in the terror stabs deep into the heart of the pre-emption element of the Bush Doctrine, taking away our right to claim the War on Terror as an act of self-defense.

HOW 24 PLAYS TO THE SUPPORTERS OF THE BUSH DOCTRINE

Obviously, though, 24 is not a massive critique of the Bush Doctrine. Many on the political right (such as Dick Cheney, Rush Limbaugh, and Michael Chertoff) call themselves huge fans of the show (Heritage Foundation). It supports a "war footing" against terror by portraying an aggressive stance against terrorism (CTU is a fictional counterterror force), and seems to support the internationalist interventionism (Bauer goes down to Mexico, had dealings in Kosovo, etc.) that the Bush Doctrine promotes.

Also, it supports the notion that the United States is constantly under siege. Each season of the show is designed around the hypothetical ticking time bomb scenario, which asks us, "If there were a nuclear bomb (or some other weapon that would kill a lot of people) that were hidden, and set to go off in minutes (or an hour, or twenty-four hours), what would you be willing to do to stop it?"—essentially, whether you would do something unethical for the sake of the greater good. The entire narrative of the show—a countdown to the last second of twenty-four hours—constantly puts the characters in situations where that very question is crucial . . . situations where Jack Bauer thrives.

The show also suggests that Jack Bauer's actions rightfully go beyond the rules of normal ethical restraints due to the circumstances and consequences of that ticking time bomb scenario. This supports the moral exceptionalism inherent in the Bush Doctrine. Innocent or guilty, Bauer tortures, mutilates, kills, and even frees suspects so that he may stop the hidden, ever-present threat. This sense of urgency in fighting terror—

because there's (always) a hidden, ticking bomb somewhere—is the very essence of that foreign policy shift the Bush Administration initiated after 9/11: we attack them only so that they cannot attack us first. Because our freedoms and way of life are under constant threat, our actions in defending ourselves are beyond reproach.

WINNER: BUSH DOCTRINE SUPPORTERS

It's difficult to say if 24's support for the Bush Doctrine outweighs its criticism. Both are present in the show, and neither side seems to have a clear advantage. The only real way to put the support and criticism into perspective is to understand that the ticking time bomb scenario (the countdown to the last minute of each show; the last second of each plot twist; the last moment of the series) is the show's essential feature, the gimmick without which the show would not be what it is.

24 supports the Bush Doctrine by building, into the very concept of the show, the threat of the utter destruction facing the United States should terrorist plots succeed. It is this threat that the Bush Doctrine uses to justify and guide our actions in the War on Terror; it is this aspect of the show that puts the show's support firmly behind the Bush Doctrine.

The hypothetical ticking time bomb scenario is more than a hypothesis in 24. It's the very world of the show. It is not a question of what you would do but a proclamation of what is done. The narrative conveys both that we are absolutely in danger (terror is everywhere) and absolutely safe (as long as we have Jack Bauer). 24 turns the hypothetical scenario into concrete reality and justifies Jack Bauer's moral exceptionalism, trumping any possible critique of the Bush Doctrine within the show. As such, the critiques of the Bush Doctrine within the show are contextualized and tamed—they are not so much moral claims by the show as a whole as they are revelations that serve the drama of the narrative. The failings of politicians and policy makers are elements of the fiction, not claims on the Bush Doctrine.

WHY EVERYONE LOVES THE SHOW ANYWAY

So, if 24 essentially supports the Bush Doctrine, why does everyone love it? Jean Baudrillard, in his book *Simulacra and Simulation*, explains the impact that media has on its audience when it simulates reality. For Baudrillard, the simulation of reality can impact the way we see the world (1). This applies to *24* as much as any other media event.

By simulating a clock-ticking, terror-filled reality, *24* makes the policies and politics of the War on Terror vital to our nation and our public discourse—even though the show's simulated reality is not, in fact, real. Jack Bauer is not real. There are no Jack Bauers in Homeland Security or the FBI. There are teams of people digging through intelligence trying to uncover terrorist plots and stopping them from happening, but no Jack Bauer. There are no ticking time bomb scenarios, let alone a ticking time bomb world. That is a hypothetical morality test, not concrete fact. Terrorists and terrorism are real, but their reality is different than the one *24* conveys. Yet, because of *24*'s success at simulating terror and conveying a terror-filled reality, those policies and politics become vital, in the minds of the *24* fan, to the continuation of our nation.

Much like the fashion designer who sells clothes by suggesting we cannot be sexy if we do not buy their brand, *24* tells us we cannot be safe after 9/11 if we do not embrace moral exceptionalism and fight the War on Terror. And like the consumer who buys the brand and then sees themselves as sexy (when, in fact, they are the same person, in the same body, as they were before), fans of *24* overlook that, in fact, America was not destroyed on 9/11. Neither our freedoms nor our way of life evaporated. But *24* premiered seven weeks after September 11, on November 6, 2001, and simulated that destruction, feeding on our fears and selling Bush's War on Terror.

By simulating terrorism, *24* creates a spectacle for the audience and becomes a way to both purge and revive our passion and fears. We're able to see terrorism defeated, but not really (since it's not the real terrorism Jack Bauer is fighting), and thus our fears are re-established, if not heightened. *24* immerses the viewer into a new, total reality—one where terror is everywhere—and reinvigorates our sense of moral exception in the real-world War on Terror. Even though *24* and the Bush Doctrine share the same central idea—that moral exceptionalism must be used in the face of the imminent threat of that ticking time bomb—the War on Terror cannot produce footage and media events that convey the all-threatening world the Bush Doctrine presumes to exist. *24* can and does.

CONCLUSION

Viewers across the political spectrum love this show because they are seduced by the absolute importance 24 gives their political debate. They all unconditionally accept the reality of Bush's War on Terror. All that is different is their ideological concerns about it—which are raised to grave importance under the shining Hollywood lights of 24. By creating a concrete reality based on the ticking time bomb scenario, that hypothetical situation suddenly becomes more important than politics as usual. It becomes real; it matters.

So what would 24 look like if it critiqued the Bush Doctrine? The Bush Doctrine suggests that al-Qaeda has the power to end our way of life and take away our freedoms; it suggests our freedoms and way of life are potentially weaker than al-Qaeda's terror. Obviously, the United States needed to increase security in the wake of September 11, 2001. Overthrowing the Taliban and attacking al-Qaeda were certainly a part of increasing global security. But the Bush Doctrine does more than enact global security measures. It suggests al-Qaeda might, in fact, remake America (and the world) in accordance with its radical ideology.

Were 24 a critique of the Bush Doctrine, it would state that America cannot be remade in accordance with that ideology, because the American people will never allow it. That America's freedoms will survive regardless of the number or size of terrorist attacks we may suffer. That our way of life and our freedoms are intrinsically stronger than al-Qaeda's terrorism. For 24 to be a true critique of the Bush Doctrine, it would need to portray Jack Bauer failing, the terrorists succeeding in their plots, and America's freedoms not being destroyed—the United States, its Constitution, and the American people still existing. Just as they did on the morning of September 12, 2001, and just as they did after every other terrorist attack al-Qaeda has attempted.

With the War on Terror continuing to escalate and the war in Iraq seemingly endless, we must wonder about the future of the United States. Will we fight a perpetual War on Terror? Will we constantly see ourselves as under threat of losing our freedoms? Will we constantly see 9/11 as the day the world changed? Or will we begin to see hope that, beyond the threats of jihadists, our way of life will not be destroyed? On September 11, America came together, and though we mourned our losses, for a moment there was a feeling of certainty that America's free-doms and way of life were far stronger than al-Qaeda and their acts of terror.

However, it's hard to recall that feeling as we sift through our memo-ries of the day and try to remove CTU, Jack Bauer, and the moral excep-tionalism *24* helps us feel so passionately about. It's so hard to see into the days after 9/11 without hearing that heart-pounding clock ticking down, without feeling the fear of utter destruction that *24* engenders, and the satisfaction at torture saving the day. Perhaps, though, if we can see a world beyond the War on Terror, a world where our way of life has not been destroyed and our freedoms have not been taken away, we will see a stronger America—one that does not fear ticking time bombs and has a confidence in itself that outshines any terrorist threat.

———————

Aaron Thomas Nelson is a writer and editor living in El Dorado Hills, California, with his wife and four daughters. Along with his graphic novel *Marlow*, his comics *Joe Doogan: Zombie Hunter* and *Kid Lightspeed and the Neutron Women* are slated for publication. He has also edited two volumes of Arcana's *Dark Horrors Anthology*. In 2005, he delivered a paper on *Ultimate Spider-Man* at Comic-Con in San Diego. When he has some spare time, Aaron enjoys running. Aaron is also found at www.aaronthomasnelson.com.

REFERENCES

Baudrilard, Jean. *Simulacra and Simulation*. Ann Arbor: The University of Michigan, 1994.

Bush, President George W. "Address to a Joint Session of Congress and the American People." *The White House* 20 Sep. 2001.

_____. "President Discusses War on Terrorism." *World Congress Center* 8 Nov. 2001.

_____. "President Discusses Patriot Act." *Ohio State Highway Patrol Academy* 9 Jun. 2005.

The Heritage Foundation, "'24' and America's Image in Fighting Terrorism:

Fact, Fiction, or Does It Matter?" *The Heritage Foundation* 23 Jun. 2006. <http://www.heritage.org/Press/Events/ev062306.cfm>

Tyler, Patrick E. "U.S. Strategy Plan Calls for Insuring No Rivals Develop a One-Superpower World." *The New York Times* nytimes.com. 8 Mar. 1992. <http://work.colum.edu/—amiller/wolfowitz1992.htm>

The White House. "The National Security Strategy of the United States of America." *The White House* 17 Sep. 2002.

The Third Degree

Uncovering the Truth in 24

CHRISTOPHER J. PATRICK AND DEBORAH L. PATRICK

W hy do individuals in society lie? What methods exist to get at the truth in cases where individuals are lying or withholding information? Is it possible to determine conclusively whether someone is being truthful or not in what they tell us? Are there limits on how far agents of the government should be allowed to go in extracting the truth from enemies such as terrorists?

The phenomenon of deception is a fascinating one, and central to the drama of *24*. For the show's protagonists, and its viewers as well, the truth seems like a moving target that is always just beyond range. In virtually every episode of every season, the truth is withheld or distorted in significant ways that threaten the safety of the public at large or specific individuals within it. Jack Bauer and his associates at CTU, in an ever-present race against time, must resort to any means necessary to uncover the truth from those bent on concealing it from them.

This essay considers, with reference to characters and dramatic scenes from *24*, the motives that people have for lying in personal and public life, and the various methods that exist for extracting the truth, ranging from verbal and behavioral analysis to physical torture. Our aim is to provide the reader with some perspective on the challenges inherent in uncovering the truth, and the merits and limitations of various techniques that have been developed to detect lies.

THE "WHYS" OF LIES: MOTIVES FOR DECEPTION

People lie for all sorts of reasons, and lying in its myriad forms is pervasive in the dealings that people have with one another. One need only imagine a world without deception of any kind to appreciate how essential lies are as a lubricant for the wheels of human interaction. At the same time, we all recognize the difference between innocuous, everyday acts of deceit (what we call "white lies") and lies that are more consequential—those generally considered to be illegal (fraud, perjury, obstruction of justice [i.e., lying to the police], and income tax evasion [i.e., lying on one's tax return]) or immoral. Generally speaking, society frowns upon acts of deception aimed at covering one's tracks or gaining the upper hand with others (e.g., lying to get out of work or other obligations; lying to get back at someone who has wronged you; lying to impress someone with whom you desire a relationship; lying to cover up an addiction). Deceptive acts of this sort can be termed *personal* lies.

Characters in the television series *24* frequently lie or conceal the truth for personal reasons. One personal motive for lying that is featured prominently is revenge. For example, the main threat in season one was a plot to assassinate Senator David Palmer and frame Jack Bauer for it, masterminded by Andre and Alexis Drazen, sons of former Serbian military commander Victor Drazen. The motive was vengeance: the Drazen brothers were seeking to avenge the deaths of family members slain two years earlier in Kosovo by a U.S. Special Operations team, commissioned by Senator Palmer and led by Jack, that was ordered to find and eliminate Victor; although Victor managed to evade the attack, his wife and daughter were killed. The Drazen brothers perpetrated numerous ongoing acts of deception to advance this conspiracy.

Two other salient personal motives for lying in *24* are greed and ambition. Two characters notable for the lengths to which they will go to attain wealth and status are Nina Myers and Jack's father, Phillip. Myers, a highly skilled liar who succeeded in duping even Jack Bauer for much of the show's first season, was introduced early in season one as an agent of CTU, but over time was revealed to be an accomplice of the Drazen family in their plot to assassinate David Palmer. The motives for her treachery were not altogether specified, but appeared to revolve around greed and personal ambition. Phillip Bauer, a ruthless corporate magnate whose sole concerns are wealth and power, was introduced in season six in connection with a terrorist plot to detonate nuclear weapons smuggled from Russia into the U.S. Phillip's greed was directly responsible for the Russian nuclear bombs falling into the hands of the terrorists. Over the course of season six, Phillip engaged in unspeakable acts of treachery and deceit, including brutally murdering his son Graem and casting the blame on Jack; coercing Graem's wife Marilyn into helping him set a trap for Jack by threatening to kill her son, Josh; providing weapons-related technology to Chinese agents that imperiled the security of Russia and the safety of the United States; and kidnapping Josh (his grandson) and forcing Josh to accompany him to China.

Personal reasons aren't, naturally, the only reason for lying, especially in *24*. Another broad motive people sometimes have for concealing or distorting the truth is because they are fulfilling a formal role or duty that calls for deceptive activity. This type of lying can be referred to as *institutional* lying. In *24*, deceptive practices are frequently used by politicians or agents of the government to preserve order and to safeguard the welfare of the public. In season six, U.S. Vice President Noah Daniels—serving as commander-in-chief following an assassination attempt on President Wayne Palmer that left Palmer in a coma—engaged in a variety of lies to advance a radical anti-terrorism policy within the U.S. (including reliance on racial profiling and forcible detention of suspects), and put pressure on an unnamed Middle Eastern government to help the U.S. stop a terrorist cell from detonating rogue nuclear weapons on American soil. Daniels's acts of deception included concealing the truth about the assassination attempt on President Palmer in order to place blame for the attempt on terrorist leader Hamri Al-Assad; convincing White House Chief of Staff Tom Lennox to advise Assad's home country that he witnessed Assad planting what he later realized to be an explosive device; lying to the U.S. people about Assad's role in the assassination attempt in a presidential address to the nation; and conspiring with his assistant Lisa Miller to have National Security Advisor Karen Hayes (an opponent of his policies) removed from service on false pretenses.

Besides lying for political reasons, characters in 24—agents of CTU and other U.S. government agencies, as well as foreign operatives—regularly engage in acts of deception for purposes of espionage or counterespionage. CTU is a fictional organization but it is similar in function to the Special Operations division of the CIA's real-life Counterterrorist Center and parallels the role of the real-life Department of Homeland Security in its mission to protect the country from terrorist attacks. Like those of its real-life counterparts, CTU's activities involve a considerable degree of stealth and deception.

In season two, for example, Jack Bauer went to extraordinary lengths to infiltrate a criminal gang headed by Joseph Wald, whom Jack believed had knowledge of the terrorist plot to detonate a nuclear bomb in Los Angeles. Bauer established a fake criminal identity for himself (including simulated police record) with help from information systems experts at CTU. He also arranged for FBI agents to transport Marshall Goren, a witness under federal protective custody scheduled to testify in a case against Wald, to CTU for the ostensible purpose of questioning him, but instead shot and then decapitated him. He then delivered Goren's head to members of Joseph Wald's gang to convince them he was a loyal associate of Wald's seeking to make contact with him.

Later in season two, Bauer undertook another chilling ruse, in order to extract information regarding the location of the nuclear bomb from Second Wave terrorist group leader Syed Ali. Bauer had Ali in custody, but Ali refused to divulge what he knew. Bauer warned Ali that U.S. government operatives in Ali's home country had captured his family and were standing ready to execute them one by one, on Bauer's orders, if Ali continued to withhold information, and presented Ali with a remote video feed of his wife and two sons, bound to chairs in the presence of armed soldiers. He repeated his warning and admonished Ali to disclose the location of the nuclear device immediately. When Ali again refused, Bauer relayed an order via cell phone for the captors to execute Ali's older son. Ali watched in horror as his son was toppled backward in his chair and executed by pistol shot just out of camera range. Ali broke down at this point and confessed to Bauer what he knew about the location of the bomb. Only afterward did Bauer reveal to Ali that the execution was in fact staged—and that both of his sons, and his wife as well, remained alive.

It should be noted that not all instances of lying fall neatly into one category versus the other. In season one, Senator David Palmer and his wife Sherry argued about whether they should take steps to conceal information from their daughter Nicole and from the public media regarding their son Keith's possible involvement in a homicide. The motives for deception in this case were both political (disclosure of this information could damage Palmer's candidacy for the presidency) and personal (disclosure could be harmful to the Palmers' children).

"JUST THE FACTS": METHODS FOR DETECTING LIES

Efforts to deceive or withhold information from others, arising from institutional and/or personal motives, constitute a major source of drama in 24. A further source of dramatic action—as well as a catalyst for public controversy regarding the series—is the methods used by agents of the U.S. government (including Jack Bauer) and their enemies to uncover the truth. What techniques exist in real life for extracting the truth from individuals who are lying or withholding information, and how are these techniques reflected in the series 24? What advantages and drawbacks are there to different methods for detecting lies or concealed information?

Formal strategies for uncovering the truth have existed since early times. One method used in ancient China was to place dry rice grains in the mouths of suspects while questioning them. Individuals who exhibited difficulty in speaking due to rice adhering to their tongues were deemed guilty, on the assumption that a dry mouth indicates fear associated with guilt or apprehension about being detected. Another method, popular in medieval Europe, was trial by ordeal—in which the accused person was subjected to a painful challenge of some kind such as immersing an arm in boiling water or walking across red-hot coals. The underlying premise, based on mystical or religious beliefs, was that a truthful person would either be spared physical injury or recover quickly from the ordeal whereas a guilty individual would exhibit immediate and persisting effects. In contemporary society, police and government agencies rely on a variety of more technically refined methods for detecting lies; many of these are featured at one point or another in 24. Here, we provide a brief overview of these various techniques, grouped

91

into three categories: behavioral analysis, physiological measurement, and interrogation.

Behavioral Analysis

One approach to detecting lies is through objective, quantitative analysis of speech or nonverbal behavior. Quantitative behavioral analysis techniques rely on signs or indicators that people use naturally, every day, to evaluate the veracity of information conveyed by others, including verbal inconsistencies, vagueness, facial tics, and other overt signs of nervousness. In 24, CTU agents routinely attend to behavioral indicators of this kind in gauging the truthfulness of suspects: late in season two, for example, Jack Bauer concludes that Marie Warner was lying about a nuclear bomb because her description of the bomb's triggering device was implausible. The difference between what you and I do when we interact with people in our daily lives and quantitative verbal and nonverbal behavioral analysis is that, in quantitative analysis, critical indicators are coded and quantified, and then compared against objective norms of some kind (i.e., expected frequencies of occurrence within non-deceptive behavioral sequences) to evaluate truthfulness.

Quantitative verbal analysis methods focus on coding variations in the content and structure of speech. Methods of this kind can be applied to written statements as well as recorded communications (e.g., Adams and Jarvis). Aspects of speech content believed to provide clues to deception include the level of detail included in narrative accounts (truthful narratives tend to contain more specific details than fabricated narratives), factual inconsistencies between statements within a narrative, and presence of emotional content (truthful narratives tend to include more descriptions of an individual's affective state at the time of events being discussed). Structural elements of speech that are considered to be indices of deception in verbal analysis include grammatical slips (e.g., inappropriate use of the pronoun "we" in describing an encounter with an abductor or assailant), shifts in tense (e.g., from past to present) across statements, long pauses in speech, and gaps in a narrative that indicate reluctance to discuss particular details.

Nonverbal behaviors can also be coded to assess for deception. The best-known review of measures of this kind is provided by psychology researcher Paul Ekman in his book *Telling Lies*. A major focus of the book is facial indicators of lying. Some of these include subtle, involuntary (micro) expressions or mixed facial expressions that indicate concealed emotional states; asymmetric (lopsided) expressions; lingering expressions; forced smiles; blushing; and excessive blinking. Manual (by an observer) and automated (computerized) procedures exist for coding facial indicators of this kind from video records. Ekman's book also describes clues to deceit that can be coded from an individual's physical movements and posture ("body language"). Indicators of this kind include involuntary communicative gestures ("emblematic slips"; e.g., shrugs); diminished frequency of actions that serve to accent speech ("illustrators"; e.g., hand movements); hand-to-face gestures; crossing of arms or legs; frequent swallowing; and lip-licking.

Available evidence indicates that objective methods of this sort are more accurate for detecting deception than subjective impressions. However, behavioral analysis techniques are far from infallible. As is true with the physiological measures described in the next section, individuals can appear deceptive in terms of what they say or do because they are upset or nervous rather than because they are untruthful. In addition, some individuals (e.g., psychopaths; see below) may be capable of lying without giving themselves away either verbally or behaviorally.

Physiological Measurement

The use of bodily response measurement to assess truthfulness is referred to as lie detector testing, or alternatively, physiological detection of deception. This approach made an appearance early in season four of *24*, when Richard Heller submitted to a lie detector test at CTU headquarters to determine whether he had knowledge of his father and sister's abduction. The oldest and best-known physiological method of lie detection (that used on Richard Heller) is polygraph testing, which utilizes measures of respiration, blood pressure, and sweat gland activity (skin resistance, or galvanic skin response [GSR]). Another approach with a long history is voice stress analysis, which relies on changes in vocal frequency (pitch) to index emotional arousal. In more recent years, direct measurement of brain reactivity, in the form of event-related potentials (ERPs) or magnetic resonance imaging (MRI) response, has been used for purposes of lie detection.

Traditional polygraphic lie detection tests are of two types: specific incident tests and screening tests. Specific incident tests are used by the police or other investigative agencies to evaluate the truthfulness of a suspect with regard to a known offense, such as a theft or murder. The specific incident test that is used most often by the police is the control question test (CQT). In this procedure, the examiner compares the suspect's physiological reactions to questions of two kinds: relevant questions, dealing with the specific incident (offense) under investigation (e.g., "On November 10, did you steal $5000 from the AAA Savings and Loan?"); and control questions, which ask about general inclinations toward wrongdoing in the suspect's past (e.g., "During the first twenty-one years of your life, did you ever take anything of value that wasn't yours?"). The theory behind the CQT is that deceptive individuals will react more strongly to the relevant questions because they know they are lying to these questions, whereas truthful individuals will react more strongly to the control questions because they are unsure about their answers to these. However, a problem with the CQT is that some suspects may respond more to the relevant questions even if innocent—because they stand accused of the crime to which these questions refer and they are nervous about failing the test. The best available evidence indicates that the standard CQT used by the police is markedly biased against innocent people (Lykken).

Another type of polygraph test, known as a screening examination, is used to probe for involvement in unspecified illicit activities. For example, an employer may use a test of this kind to ascertain whether a job candidate has a history of malfeasance that would make him a bad employment risk, or if a current employee might be engaging in activities that are detrimental to operations. The screening examination consists primarily of relevant questions covering various undesirable behaviors (e.g., "Have you ever stolen from an employer?"; "Have you engaged in drinking or drug use at work since being employed here?"). Questions that prompt large reactions in comparison with others become the focus of follow-up inquiries by the examiner to determine whether the examinee is hiding something. The outcome of the test is determined by whether incriminating disclosures are made by the examinee in response to these follow-up inquiries.

94

Available evidence indicates that the polygraph screening test, like the CQT, is biased against innocent people (i.e., individuals can react more to particular screening questions because they are nervous or indignant about being asked such questions, rather than because they are lying). Furthermore, from a civil liberties standpoint, this kind of test can be viewed as an invasion of the right of individuals to privacy in the workplace. For these reasons, polygraph screening tests were banned from use in the private sector by federal legislation, the Employee Polygraph Protection Act, passed in 1988. However, the use of polygraph screening remains permissible for job candidates and employees of law enforcement and national security agencies—under the rationale that privacy concerns must be balanced against issues of public safety in organizations of this kind. Nonetheless, screening tests remain problematic even in contexts such as these because of their known fallibility. As one powerful example, senior CIA official Aldrich Ames operated for many years as a spy for the Soviet Union despite being subjected to routine polygraph screening tests. He was ultimately exposed through standard investigative techniques, but only after his acts of betrayal had yielded disastrous consequences—including the deaths of ten CIA operatives overseas.

The Ames case highlights an intriguing question regarding the fallibility of polygraphic lie detection. Can individuals without a conscience, who lack normal feelings of guilt for their actions, pass a polygraph test even when lying? Individuals of this sort are referred to as psychopaths ("psychopathic personalities"), or sociopaths. CTU agent Nina Myers and Jack Bauer's father Phillip could be considered psychopaths; Phillip Bauer is in fact labeled a "sociopath" by government officials in season six. Certainly, traitor Aldrich Ames evidenced a number of features of a psychopathic personality, and some empirical research indicates that individuals with strong impression management skills are more likely to pass polygraph screening tests. On the other hand, compelling evidence exists that guilty psychopaths fail the control question test at rates similar to guilty non-psychopaths (Patrick and Iacono 1989). Why is it that psychopaths fail control question tests but not polygraph screening tests? Likely, two factors are involved. One is that psychopaths perceive the control question test as a game in which their job is to "fool" the examiner about a specific issue—and their investment in the game (rather than guilt) prompts them to react to the relevant questions. Ekman referred to this kind of reactivity on the part of psychopaths as "duping delight." The other factor is that psychopaths may be more able to talk their way out of enhanced reactions to particular relevant questions on a polygraph screening test, because here the outcome of the test is determined more by what the examinee says to the examiner about his or her reactions than by reactivity per se.

Lykken argued that, in general, the fallibility of traditional polygraphic lie detection derives from the fact that reactions on a polygraph test reflect emotional arousal, rather than guilt specifically. As a potential remedy for this, Lykken proposed an alternative approach to lie detection for use in specific incident investigations, the "guilty knowledge test" (GKT). The GKT is based on the idea that the person who is guilty of a crime will possess knowledge of specific information about the crime that an innocent person will not. For example, in the Nicole Simpson/Ronald Goldman murder case, the perpetrator would have known—prior to the release of crime scene details to the public—how the victims were killed, what they were wearing at the time of death, where their bodies were discovered, etc. Knowing this, case investigators could have constructed a GKT consisting of a series of questions, in multiple-choice format, regarding these sorts of details (e.g., If you are the murderer, you will know how Nicole was killed. Was she . . . [a] poisoned? [b] bludgeoned? [c] shot? [d] stabbed? [e] strangled?). For a series of six such questions, each having five options, the odds of an innocent person reacting most to the critical option on each question (e.g., to option [e] in the example given) would be vanishingly small (5^6, or 1 in 15,625). If the police had used this type of lie detector test with O. J. Simpson immediately upon apprehending him, it is likely we would now know the truth about whether he in fact did it.

The core advantage of the GKT in comparison with the control question test is that it functions to protect the innocent (i.e., because "what you don't know can't hurt you"). Consistent with this, laboratory research findings consistently indicate that innocent suspects almost never fail the GKT. Even so, and despite the fact that the GKT has existed for close to fifty years, the GKT is not used routinely by police or government agencies in the U.S. because the control question test is so well established. However, this state of affairs seems likely to change. For one thing, the GKT has achieved widespread use and proved its worth in other countries, most notably Japan. In addition, because of its unique format, the GKT has been the method of choice in newer studies that have investigated the use of ERP and MRI hemodynamic responses in the detection of deception. These methods are exciting because they rely on direct measurement of brain reactivity and because accuracy rates for these methods in laboratory studies to date have been very impressive (for a review, see Iacono and Patrick 2006).

Interrogation

Interrogation refers to formal methods of questioning used to obtain information from someone who is concealing or withholding it. Interrogation is the approach used most frequently by Jack Bauer and others on 24 to extract confessions from uncooperative or deceptive individuals. Interrogation invariably entails some degree of pressure or manipulation. This can range from simple psychological tactics designed to make it easier for the suspect to admit the truth to the induction of physical pain.

The methods that the police are allowed to use in interrogating criminal suspects are limited by the constitutional rights of individuals and the legal rules of evidence. There are several methods, however, that the police can employ, such as strategies for developing rapport, persuasive techniques, and subtle forms of deception. Techniques used to establish rapport include sympathizing with the suspect, downplaying the moral gravity of the offense, and using mild physical contact (e.g., touching the suspect's shoulder or hand). Persuasive methods include flattering the suspect, calling attention to behaviors in the interview that signal guilt, and confronting the suspect with known incriminating evidence. Deceptive tactics include bluffing (e.g., regarding known details of the offense, or the suspect's activities) and use of the so-called "good cop/bad cop" routine (i.e., in which two officers, one friendly and the other unfriendly, alternate in interrogating the individual in order to establish an alliance with the friendly officer that encourages cooperation).

Another approach to interrogation, "assisted interrogation," involves the use of mind-altering chemicals ("truth drugs") or hypnosis to enhance an examinee's susceptibility to instruction and willingness to divulge information. The best-known truth drug is Sodium Pentothal (generic name sodium thiopental), a fast-acting barbiturate depressant also used, in higher doses, as a general anesthetic. Other drugs of this sort include scopolamine and ethanol (pure alcohol). The dubious premise behind the use of sedative agents like these is that their suppressant effect on higher cortical functioning leads to disinhibition of thought and speech, and heightened candor. In fact, while available evidence indicates that individuals do tend to talk more under the influence of sedative drugs, it is not necessarily the case that they are more truthful. Moreover, there is evidence that heightened states of suggestibility, associated with drug intoxication or hypnosis, can facilitate the formation of false memories. For this reason, information obtained from a suspect or eyewitness while under the influence of a truth drug or hypnosis is not generally admissible in court.

Hypnosis is a state of altered awareness and heightened suggestibility induced through guided attention and relaxation. Because the process requires the subject's participation, the use of hypnosis for purposes of interrogation tends to be limited to cases in which an individual is cooperative but unable to recall critical details of an incident due to amnesia, forgetting, or inattention at the time of its occurrence—for example, to aid an eyewitness in remembering information about a crime. However, because of the potential for falsification with hypnotically enhanced memories, it is advisable to independently corroborate information obtained through hypnosis before drawing conclusions in cases where something important is at stake.

In 24, more extreme forms of interrogation are used by Jack Bauer and other agents of CTU, with the rationale that radical methods are warranted in circumstances where information must be obtained in order to save lives. The most controversial interrogation strategy featured in 24— one that has led to public outcries from U.S. government officials and civil rights groups—is torture. Although seasons one through five included interrogation scenes involving physical coercion and torture, scenes of this kind ascended to new levels in season six. This season began with Jack Bauer's release after enduring twenty months of intensive torture in a Chinese prison. In subsequent episodes, Jack showed he was ready and willing to engage in torture-based interrogation himself to obtain information from individuals linked to the terrorist nuclear threat he was fighting to stop. In episode six, Jack asphyxiated his brother Graem using a plastic bag to get him to divulge where their father Phillip was, and in episode seven he injected Graem with progressively higher doses of the (fictional) pain-inducing drug hyoscine-pentothal to compel Graem to admit what he knew about the nuclear conspiracy. Later in season six, Jack subjected Russian consul Anatoly Markov to a brutal interrogation in which he severed one of Markov's fingers with a cigar clipper. In episode seventeen, Bauer and fellow agent Mike Doyle took turns bludgeoning terrorist leader Abu Fayed and threatening to shoot him in order to learn what he knew about the location of the rogue nuclear weapons.

Along with "third degree" tactics of this kind, CTU agents and terrorist operatives also rely on threats toward other people in order to persuade suspects to talk. This approach tends to be used after interrogation efforts and physical coercion directed at the suspect fail. As described earlier, Jack Bauer threatened the family of terrorist Syed Ali in season two to induce him to talk because Bauer could see that direct intimidation and torture would be ineffective with Ali. In season three, Bauer ordered bioterrorist Stephen Saunders's daughter dragged into a virus-infected building to compel Saunders to reveal what he knew about the location of additional vials of the deadly virus. In season six, the president himself instructed officials in Fayed's home country to execute General Habib's son in Habib's presence if Habib did not call and lie to Fayed.

Interrogation techniques of this sort, entailing physical or psychological brutality, have serious drawbacks. Most obviously, these methods are unethical and inhumane. What is it about threats or depictions of physical pain and suffering in particular that evoke such powerful feelings in all of us? There are of course many perspectives on this, but one of the most intriguing comes from modern neurobiological research on the nature and bases of human emotion. Research of this kind has revealed that survival-related instincts, including fears of suffering and death, are hardwired into basic neural structures of the brain—in particular, structures comprising the brain's limbic system. One key limbic structure is the amygdala, believed to govern fear reactivity and fear learning (LeDoux). In humans, visual depictions of threat (aimed weapons, attackers) and mutilated limbs or bodies are especially effective in evoking fear reactions associated with amygdala activation (Bradley,

Codispoti, Cuthbert, and Lang). From this standpoint, threats of death or dismemberment trigger emotional reactions of the most primal sort—reactions that arise from the instinctual core of an individual and completely overwhelm reason and dignity.

While it might be argued that inhumane methods are sometimes necessary to combat inhumane activities such as terrorism or genocide, compelling political and practical counterarguments exist. One prominent political counterargument is that the use of such methods by nations like the U.S. opens the door to their use by other nations and groups around the world. Incidents like the Abu Ghraib scandal of 2004, which prompted the U.S. Senate to pass new legislation governing the treatment of military detainees, serve as a reminder of the need for limits on how even our most ruthless enemies are treated. A key practical counterargument is that punitive interrogation methods create a heightened potential for false confessions by innocent suspects. Faced with the prospect of protracted suffering, mutilation, or death—and overwhelmed by the deep-rooted feelings of terror that threats of this kind arouse—how many of us would cling to a truthful denial rather than admit to whatever our accusers demanded of us?

TRUTH AND LIES: THE FINAL WORD

The real-life search for reliable methods to uncover the truth has been—and seems likely to remain—a perpetual quest. In cases where the facts of a crime are known, but no suspect is willing to confess, Lykken's guilty knowledge test may offer the best available strategy for determining the "Who." The prospects for success with this technique are likely to be enhanced by continued research focusing on direct brain measurement and by work that advances our understanding of basic processes underlying memory and its retrieval. On the other hand, in situations where essential facts are unknown and the focus is on establishing the "What," "When," "Why," or "How"—as is frequently the case in 24—other methods need to be considered. What method should investigators turn to in cases like this, particularly when failure is certain to have devastating consequences and the seconds are ticking relentlessly away? The answer is far from clear. However, from an ethical and scientific standpoint, one thing is clear: torture is not the answer.

CHRISTOPHER J. PATRICK, PH.D., is Hathaway Professor of Psychology and director of clinical training at the University of Minnesota, where his teaching and research interests focus on emotional and cognitive aspects of crime, violence, antisocial personality, and psychopathic behavior. He is president of the Society for Scientific Study of Psychopathy, and a recipient of early scientific career awards from the American Psychological Association and the Society for Psychophysiological Research. Beyond the office, his activities include parenting, fiction reading and writing, cooking, softball, ocean surfing, and guitar playing.

DEBORAH L. PATRICK worked for years as a legal professional and elementary school teacher. In addition to being an avid fan of *24*, her passions include her daughter Sarah, decorating and home remodeling, horticulture, art, music, yoga, and travel. This is her first published work.

REFERENCES

Adams, Susan H. and John P. Jarvis, "Indicators of Veracity and Deception: An Analysis of Written Statements Made to Police," *International Journal of Speech, Language and the Law* 13 (2006): 1-22.

Bradley, Margaret M., Maurizio Codispoti, Bruce N. Cuthbert, and Peter J. Lang, "Emotion and Motivation I: Defensive and Appetitive Reactions in Picture Processing," *Emotion* 1 (2001): 276-298.

Ekman, Paul. *Telling Lies* (2ⁿᵈ ed.). New York: W. W. Norton & Co., 2001.

Iacono, William G., and Christopher J. Patrick, "Polygraph ("lie detector") Testing: Current Status and Emerging Trends." In: Weiner, Irving B. and Hess, Allen K. (Eds.), *The Handbook of Forensic Psychology*. Hoboken, NJ: John Wiley & Sons, 2006, pp. 552-588.

LeDoux, Joseph E. *The Emotional Brain*. New York: Simon & Schuster, 1996.

Lykken, David T. *A Tremor in the Blood: Uses and Abuses of the Lie Detector* (2ⁿᵈ ed.). New York: Plenum, 1998.

Christopher J. Patrick and William G. Iacono, "Psychopathy, Threat, and Polygraph Test Accuracy," *Journal of Applied Psychology* 74 (1989): 347-355.

24 and the Use of Torture to Obtain Preventive Intelligence

ALAN M. DERSHOWITZ

There are few more divisive, emotional, and contentious issues than torture. Until 9/11 the very word "torture" was regarded as a taboo. Torture was thought of as a discredited throwback to the dark ages, Nazism, Stalinism, and the Argentine Junta. We knew, of course, that it was practiced by tyrants like Saddam Hussein. But certainly not by the good guys! Then, suddenly, everything seemed to change, as the world confronted the specter of mass-casualty suicide terrorism. Such religiously motivated mayhem could not realistically be deterred by the threat of after-the-fact punishment, because the perpetrators welcomed death. Nor could we afford to wait until the crime had occurred, since the devastation would be so great. We had to instead seek to prevent or pre-empt the terrorist threat. And that is precisely what our government—for better or worse—has been doing since 9/11.

As we move closer to the "preventive state," real-time information becomes increasingly important. One mechanism for securing preventive intelligence information is interrogation. This mechanism may range from polite questioning to extreme pressure. That is where torture comes into play. The question of whether to use torture against a suspected terrorist in

103

an effort to prevent an imminent mass-casualty attack has become known as the "ticking bomb" problem. This conundrum has been placed on the world's agenda by real events, such as the terrorist attacks in NYC, DC, London, Madrid, Bali, Tel Aviv, and Baghdad. It has received widespread popular attention through television—particularly the show *24*—and it has become a source of considerable academic debate.

Little can be done to reduce the frequency of actual torture being done today because we know so little about it. It is carried out by field operatives, with plausible (or sometimes implausible) deniability at the very top. When former CIA director George Tenet was asked about this troubling subject, he stated categorically that "we do not torture." When pressed as to whether this prohibition included "water boarding"—a technique employed against Sheik Khalid Mohammed that involves near-drowning experiences—he refused to answer on the grounds that he could not discuss specific techniques. "Don't ask, don't tell" seems to be the policy.

Some argue, however, that the portrayal of torture in the media, particularly by *24*, tends to legitimize or even normalize a barbaric practice that violates both law and morality. There can be little doubt that since 9/11, torture has been shown more frequently and more positively on television than ever before. According to the Parents Television Council, which monitors such things, there were 624 portrayals of torture between 2002 and 2005, as compared with only 102 between 1996 and 2001. "The primary offender is *24*, with sixty-seven scenes in the first four seasons" (Shister). What is more disturbing to some critics is that the American hero is the torturer, thus making it seem more acceptable. A writer for the *New York Times* poses the following questions:

> Has *24* descended down a slippery slope in portraying acts of torture as normal and therefore justifiable? Is its audience, and the public more generally, also reworking the rules of war to the point where the most expedient response to terrorism is to resort to terror? In the world beyond the show, that debate remains heated. How it plays out on *24* may say a great deal about what sort of society we are in the process of becoming. (Green)

Similar questions have been raised about my controversial proposal for a torture warrant in ticking bomb cases. I have argued that, although as a personal matter of morality I oppose torture, I recognize that it is being widely used today and would be used by *every* democratic nation in a real "ticking bomb" situation. This fact leads me to argue that torture should never be authorized without a warrant signed by a responsible high-ranking authority such as the president or the chief justice. Field operatives, such as the fictional Jack Bauer, should never be allowed to use this unlawful, immoral, and extraordinary measure without express advanced approval (or in extreme emergencies, immediate after-the-fact approval). Democracy requires visibility and accountability, which is currently lacking when it comes to torture.

Before the advent of 24, I used contrived hypothetical situations to force my students to think about making difficult, even "tragic" choices. The students invariably tried to resist these tragic choices by stretching their ingenuity to come up with alternative—and less tragic—options. The classic hypothetical case involves the train engineer whose brakes become inoperative. There is no way he can stop his speeding vehicle of death. He can either do nothing, in which case he will plow into a group of school children playing on the tracks, or he can swerve onto another track on which he sees a drunk lying on the rails. (Neither decision will endanger him or his passengers.) There is no third choice. What should he do?

Whenever I present this "hypo" to my students, they seek, as any good lawyer should, to avoid the evils of either choice. They desperately try to break out of the rigid constraints of the hypothetical train situation by ascribing to the engineer a superman-like ability to drive the train off the tracks. When I force them back onto the tracks of my hypothetical, they groan in frustration.

Students love to debate positive choices: good, better, best. They don't mind moderately negative choices: bad, worse, worst. They hate tragic choices: unthinkable versus inconceivable. The kind shown on 24!

Rational decision theory teaches us how to choose among reasonable alternatives—good and bad—on a cost-benefit basis or on the basis of assigning weights to various alternatives. It does not teach us how to choose among unreasonable alternatives, each so horrible that our mind rebels even at the notion of thinking about the evil options.

Before September 11, 2001, no one thought the issue of torture would ever reemerge as a topic of serious debate in this country. Yet shortly after that watershed event, FBI agents began to leak stories suggesting that they might have to resort to torture in order to get some detainees to provide information necessary to prevent future terrorism. An FBI source told the press that, because "we are known for humanitarian treatment" of suspects, we have been unable to get any terrorist suspects to divulge information about possible future plans. "We're into this thing for thirty-five days and nobody is talking," he said in obvious frustration. "Basically we're stuck." A senior FBI aide warned that "it could get to the spot where we could go to pressure . . . where *we won't have a choice*, and we are probably getting there" (Wheeler). But in a democracy there is *always* a choice. The question is, who is authorized to make that difficult choice?

Since *24* went on the air, I have not had to construct abstract hypotheticals. The writers of *24* have created realistic—if sometimes extreme—scenarios in which the choice is between allowing large numbers of innocent civilians to die or doing unspeakable things to small numbers of probably (but not always certainly) guilty terrorists.

In one second-season episode, Jack Bauer allowed a wounded female terrorist to suffer without pain relief unless she revealed the whereabouts of a bomb. (This scenario is based on a real-life situation in which a wounded terrorist was denied pain medication.).

In another second-season episode, a terrorist who feared neither death nor torture was threatened with the execution of his entire family. When he remained silent, his son was shot before his very eyes (via satellite television). Only after he disclosed the crucial information did we learn that the shooting was faked. (This scenario could very well have been borrowed from my 1999 novel *Just Revenge*.)

In a similar scenario in season three, a terrorist who planted weaponized viruses disclosed their location only after Jack Bauer threatened to expose the terrorist's teenage daughter to the deadly virus.

Then there are the less creative scenes in which Bauer simply shoots terrorists—and in one case, a suspect's wife—in the leg and threatens to do it again.

The viewer is exposed to Bauer's thinking process, as he weighs the costs and benefits. In the virus episode, the terrorist objected to his daughter being exposed because she was innocent. So, Jack replied, were the people who would die from the virus.

The writers of 24 have been criticized for presenting these choices and resolving them in favor of doing whatever it takes. Even raising the option of torture, it is argued, breaks an important taboo.

I too have been criticized for even discussing the issue, on the ground that academic discussion confers legitimacy on a practice that deserves none. I have also been criticized for raising a "red herring," since it is "well known" that torture does not work—it produces many false confessions and useless misinformation, because a person will say anything to stop being tortured.

This argument is reminiscent of the ones made by my students desperately seeking to avoid the choice between two evils by driving the hypothetical railroad train off the track. The tragic reality is that torture sometimes works, much though many people wish it did not. There are numerous instances in which torture has produced self-proving, truthful information that was necessary to prevent harm to civilians. The *Washington Post* has recounted a case from 1995 in which Philippine authorities tortured a terrorist into disclosing information that may have foiled plots to assassinate the Pope and to crash eleven commercial airliners carrying approximately 4,000 passengers into the Pacific Ocean, as well as a plan to fly a private Cessna filled with explosives into CIA headquarters. For sixty-seven days, intelligence agents beat the suspect "with a chair and long piece of wood [breaking most of his ribs], forced water into his mouth, and crushed lit cigarettes into his private parts"— a procedure that the Philippine intelligence service calls "tactical interrogation" ("The Bojinka Plot"). After successfully employing this procedure they turned him over to American authorities, along with the life-saving information they had beaten out of him. During World War II, the Gestapo tortured members of the French Resistance into disclosing the locations of their colleagues.

It is impossible to avoid the difficult moral dilemma of choosing among evils by denying the empirical reality that torture *sometimes* works, even if it does not *always* work. No technique of crime prevention always works.

It is also sometimes argued that even when torture does produce accurate information that helps to foil a terrorist plot—as the Philippine torture did—there is no hard evidence that the *total* amount of terrorism is thereby reduced. The foiling of any one plot may simply result in the planning of another terrorist act, especially given the unlimited reservoir of potential suicide terrorists. This argument may have some merit in regard to recurring acts of retail terrorism, such as the suicide bombings in Israel. Preventing one bombing may not significantly reduce the total number of civilian deaths, though it does, of course, make a difference to those who would have been killed in the thwarted explosion. But the argument is much weaker when it comes to acts of mega-terrorism, such as those prevented by the Philippine torture or the attacks perpetrated on September 11, 2001. It is the prospect of such mega-acts—and the possibility of preventing them—that raises the stakes in the torture debate.

It is precisely because torture sometimes does work and can sometimes prevent major disasters that it still exists in many parts of the world and has been totally eliminated from none. It also explains why the U.S. government sometimes "renders" terrorist suspects to nations like Egypt and Jordan, "whose intelligence services have close ties to the CIA and where [suspects] can be subjected to interrogation tactics—including torture and threats to families—that are illegal in the United States," as the *Washington Post* has reported. "In some cases, U.S. intelligence agents remain closely involved in the interrogation. . . . 'After September 11, these sorts of movements have been occurring all of the time,' a U.S. diplomat said. 'It allows us to get information from terrorists in a way we can't do on U.S. soil'" (Grey). As former CIM counter-intelligence Chief Vincent Cannistraro observed, "Egyptian jails are full of guys with missing toenails and fingernails" ("We Have Ways to Make Them Talk"). Our government has a "don't ask, don't tell" policy when it comes to obtaining information from other governments that practice torture. All such American complicity in foreign torture violates the plain language of the Geneva Convention against torture, which explicitly prohibits torture from being inflicted not only by signatory nations but also "at the instigation of, or with the consent or acquiescence of" any person "acting in an official capacity" ("Convention against Torture"). As we began to come to grip with the horrible evils of mass murder by terrorists, it became inevitable that torture would return to the agenda, and it has. We must be prepared to think about the alternatives in a rational manner. We cannot evade our responsibility by pretending that torture is not being used or by having others use it for our benefit.

The arguments in favor of using torture as a last resort to prevent a bomb from exploding and killing many people are both simple and simple-minded. Bentham constructed a compelling hypothetical case to support his utilitarian argument against an absolute prohibition on torture:

> Suppose an occasion were to arise, in which a suspicion is entertained, as strong as that which would be received as a sufficient ground for arrest and commitment as for felony—a suspicion that at this very time a considerable number of individuals are actually suffering, by illegal violence inflictions equal in intensity to those which if inflicted by the hand of justice, would universally be spoken of under the name of torture. For the purpose of rescuing from torture these hundred innocents, should any scruple be made of applying equal or superior torture, to extract the requisite information from the mouth of one criminal, who having it in his power to make known the place where at this time the enormity was practicing or about to be practiced, should refuse to do so? To say nothing of wisdom, could any pretence be made so much as to the praise of blind and vulgar humanity, by the man who to save one criminal, should determine to abandon 100 innocent persons to the same fate? (Twining and Twining 348)

If the torture of one guilty person would be justified to prevent the torture of 100 innocent persons, it would seem to follow—certainly to Bentham—that it would also be justified to prevent the murder of thousands of innocent civilians in the ticking bomb case.

Consider two hypothetical situations that are not, unfortunately, beyond the realm of possibility. Indeed, they are both extrapolations on actual situations we have faced.

Several weeks before September 11, 2001, the Immigration and Nationalization Service detained Zacarias Moussaoui after flying instructors reported suspicious statements Moussaoui had made while seeking flying lessons. The government decided not to seek a warrant to search his computer. Now imagine they had, and discovered that he was part of a plan to destroy large occupied buildings, but without any further details. They interrogate him, give him immunity from prosecution, offer him large cash rewards and a new identity. He refuses to talk. They then threaten him, try to trick him, and employ every lawful technique available to them. He still refuses. They even inject him with Sodium Pentothal and other truth serums, but to no avail. The attack now appears to be imminent, but the FBI still has no idea what its target is or what means will be used to attack it. We cannot simply evacuate all buildings indefinitely. An FBI agent proposes the use of non-lethal torture — say, a sterilized needle inserted under the nails to produce unbearable pain without any threat to health or life, or a dental drill through an anaesthetized tooth made infamous in the film *Marathon Man*.

The simple cost-benefit analysis for employing such non-lethal torture seems overwhelming; it is surely better to inflict non-lethal pain on one guilty terrorist who is illegally withholding information needed to prevent an act of terrorism than to permit a large number of innocent victims to die (it is illegal to withhold relevant information from a grand jury after receiving immunity). Pain is a lesser and more remediable harm than death, and the lives of a thousand innocent people should be valued more than the bodily integrity of one guilty person.

If the variation on the Moussaoui case is not sufficiently compelling to make this point, we can always raise the stakes. Several weeks after September 11, our government received reports that a ten kiloton nuclear weapon may have been stolen from Russia and was on its way to New York City where it would be detonated and kill hundreds of thousands of people. The reliability of the source, code named Dragonfire, was uncertain, but assume for purposes of this hypothetical extension of the actual case, that the source was a captured terrorist — like the one tortured by the Philippine authorities — who knew precisely how and where the weapon was being bought into New York and was to be detonated. Again, everything short of torture is tried, but to no avail. It is not absolutely certain torture will work, but it is our last, best hope for preventing a cataclysmic nuclear devastation in a city too large to evacuate in time. Should non-lethal torture be tried? Bentham would certainly have said yes.

The strongest argument against any resort to torture, even in the ticking bomb case, also derives from Bentham's utilitarian calculus. Experience has shown that if torture, which has been deemed illegitimate by the civilized world for more than a century, were now to be legitimated—even for limited use in one extraordinary type of situation—such legitimation would constitute an important symbolic setback in the worldwide campaign against torture. Inevitably, the legitimation of torture by the world's leading democracy would provide a welcome justification for its more widespread use in other parts of the world. As W.L. and P.E. Twining argued in response to Bentham's support for torture even in an extremely limited category of cases:

> [T]here is at least one good practical reason for drawing a distinction between justifying an isolated act of torture in an extreme emergency of the kind postulated above and justifying the *institutionalization* of torture as a regular practice. The circumstances are so extreme in which most of us would be prepared to justify resort to torture, if at all, the conditions we would impose would be so stringent, the practical problems of devising and enforcing adequate safeguards so difficult and the risks of abuse so great that it would be unwise and dangerous to entrust any government, however enlightened, with such a power. Even an out-and-out utilitarian can support an absolute prohibition against institutionalized torture on the ground that no government in the world can be trusted not to abuse the power and to satisfy in practice the conditions he would impose. (Twining and Twining 348–349)

Bentham's own justification was based on *case* or *act* utilitarianism—a demonstration that in a *particular case*, the benefits that would flow from the limited use of torture would outweigh its costs. The argument against any use of torture would derive from *rule* utilitarianism—which considers the implications of establishing a precedent that would inevitably be extended beyond its limited case utilitarian justification to other possible evils of lesser magnitude. Even terrorism itself could be justified by a case utilitarian approach. Surely one could come up with a singular situation in which the targeting of a small number of civilians could be thought necessary to save thousands of other civilians—blowing up a German kindergarten by the relatives of inmates in a Nazi death camp, for example, and threatening to repeat the targeting of German children unless the death camps were shut down.

The reason this kind of single case utilitarian justification is simpleminded is that it has no inherent limiting principle. If non-lethal torture of one person is justified to prevent the killing of many innocent people, then what if it were necessary to use lethal torture—or at least torture which posed a substantial risk of death? What if it were necessary to torture the suspect's mother or children in order to get him to divulge the information? What if it took threatening to kill his family, his friends, his entire village? (To demonstrate that this is not just in the realm of the hypothetical, see Bob Drogin and Greg Miller, "Spy Agencies Questions of Tactics," *Los Angeles Times*, August 28, 2001: "The former CIA officer said he also suggested the agency begin targeting close relatives of known terrorists and use them to obtain intelligence. 'You get their mothers and their brothers and their sisters under your complete control, and then you make that known to the target,' he said. 'You imply or you directly threaten [that] his family is going to pay the price if he makes the wrong decision.'")

Under a simple-minded quantitative case utilitarianism, anything goes as long as the number of people tortured or killed does not exceed the number who would be saved. This is morality by numbers, unless there are other constraints on what we can properly do. These other constraints can come from rule utilitarianism or other principles of morality, such as the prohibition against deliberately punishing the innocent. Unless we are prepared to impose limits on the use of torture or other barbaric tactics that might be of some use in preventing terrorism, we risk hurling down the slippery slope into the abyss of amorality and ultimately tyranny. Dostoevsky captured the complexity of this dilemma when he had Ivan pose the following question to Alyosha in *The Brothers Karamazov*: "[I]magine that you are creating a fabric of human destiny with the object of making men happy in the end, giving them peace at least, but that it was essential and inevitable to torture to death only one tiny creature—that baby beating its breast with its fist, for instance—and to found that edifice on its unavenged tears, would you consent to be the architect on those conditions? Tell me the truth" (321).

A willingness to kill an innocent child suggests a willingness to do anything to achieve a necessary result. Hence the slippery slope. The writers of 24 have refused to slide down that slope. Whenever they have Bauer threaten to kill an innocent child, the threat is not actually carried out. Even in the world of fiction, there are lines not crossed.

It does not necessarily follow from the understandable fear of the slippery slope that we can never consider the use of non-lethal pain infliction, if its use were to be limited by acceptable principles of morality. After all, imprisoning a witness who refuses to testify after being given immunity is designed to be punitive. Such imprisonment can, on occasion, produce more pain and greater risk of death than non-lethal torture. Yet we continue to threaten and use the pain of imprisonment to loosen the tongues of reluctant witnesses. (One of my clients, who refused to testify against the mafia, was threatened by the government that if he persisted in his refusal the government would "leak" false information that he was cooperating, thus exposing him to mob retaliation.)

Indeed, it is commonplace for police and prosecutors to threaten recalcitrant suspects with prison rape. As one prosecutor put it, "[Y]ou're going to be the boyfriend of a very bad man . . ." (*USA v. Cobb*). The slippery slope is an argument of caution, not a debate stopper, since virtually every compromise with an absolutist approach to rights carries the risk of slipping further. An appropriate response to the slippery slope is to build in a principled break. For example, if non-lethal torture were legally limited to convicted terrorists who had knowledge of future massive terrorist acts, and who were given immunity and still refused to provide the information, there might still be objections to the use of torture, but they would have to go beyond the slippery slope argument.

The case-utilitarian argument for torturing a ticking bomb terrorist is bolstered by an argument from analogy—a *fortiori* argument. What moral principle could justify the death penalty for past individual murders, while condemning non-lethal torture to prevent future mass murders? Bentham posed this rhetorical question as support for his argument. The death penalty is, of course, reserved for convicted murderers. But again, what if torture were limited to convicted terrorists who refused to divulge information about future terrorism? Consider as well the analogy to the use of deadly force against suspects fleeing from arrest for dangerous felonies of which they had not yet been convicted. Or military retaliations that produce the predictable and inevitable collateral killing of some innocent civilians. The case against torture, when made by a Quaker who opposes the death penalty, war, self-defense, and the use of lethal force against fleeing felons, is understandable. But for anyone who justifies killing on the basis of a cost benefit analysis, the case against the use of non-lethal torture to save multiple lives is more difficult to make. In the end the absolute opposition to torture—even non-lethal torture in the ticking bomb case—may rest more on historical and aesthetic than moral or logical considerations.

In debating the issue of torture, the first question I am often asked is, "Do you want to take us back to the Middle Ages?" The association between any form of torture and gruesome death is powerful in the minds of most people knowledgeable of the history of its abuses. Torturing enemies "to death" was a common punishment in the bad old days. This understandable association makes it difficult for many people to think about non-lethal torture as a life *saving* technique.

The second question I am asked is, "What kind of torture do you have in mind?" When I respond by describing the sterilized needle being shoved under the fingernails, the reaction is visceral and often visible—a shudder coupled with a facial gesture of disgust. Discussions of the death penalty on the other hand can be conducted without these kinds of reactions, especially now that we literally put the condemned prisoner "to sleep" by laying him out on a gurney and injecting a lethal substance into his body. There is no breaking of the neck, burning of the brain, bursting of the internal organs, or gasping for breath that used to accompany hanging, electrocution, shooting, and gassing. The executioner has been replaced by the paramedical technician, as the aesthetics of death have become more acceptable. All this tends to cover up the reality that death is forever while non-lethal pain is temporary. In our modern age death is underrated, while pain is overrated.

I observed a similar phenomenon several years ago during the debate over corporal punishment that was generated by the decision of a Singapore court to sentence a young American to medically supervised lashes with a cane. Americans who support the death penalty and who express little concern about inner-city prison conditions were outraged by the specter of a few welts on the buttocks of an American. It was an utterly irrational display of hypocrisy and double standards. Given a

114

choice between medically administrated lashes and one month in a typical state lockup or prison, any rational and knowledgeable person would choose the lashes. No one dies of welts or pain, but many inmates of American prisons are raped, beaten, knifed, and otherwise mutilated and tortured. The difference is that we don't see—and don't want to see—what goes on behind the high walls of our prisons. Nor do we want to think about it. Raising the issue of torture makes Americans think about a brutalizing and unaesthetic phenomenon that has been out of our consciousness for many years.

The debate over the use of torture goes back many years, with Bentham supporting it in a limited category of cases, Kant opposing it as part of his categorical imperative against improperly using people as means for achieving noble ends, and Voltaire's views on the matter being "hopelessly confused" (Voltaire generally opposed torture but favored it in some cases) (Langbein 68). The modern resort to terrorism has renewed the debate over how a rights-based society should respond to the prospect of using non-lethal torture in the ticking bomb situation. In the late 1980s the Israeli government appointed a commission headed by a retired Supreme Court justice to look into precisely that situation. The commission concluded that there are "three ways for solving this grave dilemma between the vital need to preserve the very existence of the state and its citizens, and maintain its character as a law-abiding state." The first is to allow the security services to continue to fight terrorism in "a twilight zone which is outside the realm of the law." The second is "the way of the hypocrites: they declare that they abide by the rule of law, but turn a blind eye to what goes on beneath the surface." And the third, "the truthful road of the rule of law," is that "the law itself must insure a proper framework for the activity" of the security services in seeking to prevent terrorist acts ("Symposium").

There is, of course, a fourth road: namely to forgo any use of torture and simply allow the preventable terrorist act to occur. After the Supreme Court of Israel outlawed the use of physical pressure, the Israeli security services claimed that, as a result of the Supreme Court's decision, at least one preventable act of terrorism had been allowed to take place, one that killed several people when a bus was bombed. Whether this claim is true, false, or somewhere in between is difficult to assess. But it is clear that if the preventable act of terrorism was of a magnitude of the attacks of September 11, there would be a great outcry in any democracy that had deliberately refused to take available preventive action, even if it required the use of torture. During numerous public appearances since September 11, 2001, I have asked audiences for a show of hands as to how many would support the use of non-lethal torture in a ticking bomb case. Virtually every hand is raised. The few that remain down go up when I ask how many believe that torture would actually be used in such a case.

Law enforcement personnel give similar responses. This can be seen in reports of physical abuse directed against some suspects that have been detained following September 11, reports that have been taken quite seriously by at least one federal judge. (Osama Awadallah, a green-card holder living in San Diego, has made various charges of torture, abuse, and denial of access to a lawyer. Shira Scheindlin, a federal district court judge in New York, has confirmed the seriousness and credibility of the charges, saying Awadallah may have been "unlawfully arrested, unlawfully searched, abused by law enforcement officials, denied access to his lawyer and family" (Lewis). That torture is used is confirmed by the willingness of U.S. law enforcement officials to facilitate the torture of terrorist suspects by repressive regimes allied with our intelligence agencies. As one former CIA operative with thirty years of experience reported, "A lot of people are saying we need someone who can pull fingernails out. Others are saying 'Let others use interrogation methods that we don't use.' The only question then is, do you want to have CIA people in the room?" (Maccoy 111). The real issue, therefore, is not whether some torture would or would not be used in the ticking bomb case—it would. The question is whether it would be done openly, pursuant to a previously established legal procedure, or whether it would be done secretly, in violation of existing law. (My colleague Philip Heymann is the only person I have debated thus far who is willing to take the position that no form of torture should ever be permitted—or used—even if thousands of lives could be saved by its use. Whether he would act on that principled view if he were the responsible government official who was authorized to make this life-and-death choice—as distinguished from an academic with the luxury of expressing views without being accountable for their consequences—is a more difficult question. He has told me that he probably would authorize torture in an actual ticking bomb case, but that it would be wrong and he would expect to be punished for it.)

Several important values are pitted against each other in this conflict. The first is the safety and security of a nation's citizens. Under the ticking bomb scenario, this value may require the use of torture, if that were the only way to prevent the ticking bomb from exploding and killing large numbers of civilians. The second value is the preservation of civil liberties and human rights. This value requires that we not accept torture as a legitimate part of our legal system. In my debates with two prominent civil libertarians (Floyd Abrams and Harvey Silverglate), both acknowledged that they would want non-lethal torture to be used if it could prevent thousands of deaths, but they did not want torture to be officially recognized by our legal system. As Floyd Abrams put it, "In a democracy, sometimes it is necessary to do things off the books and below the radar screen." Former presidential candidate Alan Keyes took the position that although torture might be *necessary* in a given situation, it could never be *right*. He suggested that a president *should* authorize the torturing of a ticking bomb terrorist, but that this act should not be legitimated by the courts or incorporated into our legal system. He argued that wrongful and indeed unlawful acts might sometimes be necessary to preserve the nation, but that no aura of legitimacy should be placed on these actions by judicial imprimatur.

This understandable approach is in conflict with the third important value: namely, open accountability and visibility in a democracy. "Off the book actions" that are "below the radar screen" are antithetical to the theory and practice of democracy. Citizens cannot approve or disapprove of governmental actions of which they are unaware. We have learned the lesson of history that off the book actions can produce terrible consequences. Former President Nixon's creation of a group of "plumbers" led to Watergate and former President Reagan's authorization of an "off the books" foreign policy in Central America led to the Iran-Contra scandal. And these are only the ones we know about!

Perhaps the most extreme example of this hypocritical approach to torture comes — not surprisingly — from the French experience in Algeria. The French army used torture extensively in seeking to prevent terrorism during France's brutal war between 1955 and 1957. An officer who supervised this torture, General Paul Aussaresses, wrote an account of what he had done and seen, including the torture of dozens of Algerians. "The best way to make a terrorist talk when he refused to say what he knew was to torture him," he boasted (Aussaresses). Although the book was published decades after the war was over, the general was prosecuted—but not for what he had *done* to the Algerians. Instead, he was prosecuted for *revealing* what he had done, and seeking to justify it.

In a democracy governed by a rule of law, we should never want our soldiers or president to take any action that we deem wrong or illegal. A good test of whether an action should or should not be done is whether we are prepared to have it disclosed—perhaps not immediately, but certainly after some time has passed. No legal system operating under the rule of law should ever tolerate an "off the books" approach to necessity. Even the defense of necessity must be justified lawfully. The road to tyranny has always been paved with claims of necessity made by those responsible for the security of a nation. Our system of checks and balances requires that all presidential actions, like all legislative or military actions, be consistent with governing law. If it is necessary to torture in the ticking bomb case, then our governing laws must accommodate this practice. If we refuse to change our law to accommodate any particular action then our government should not take that action.

Only in a democracy committed to civil liberties would a triangular conflict of this kind exist. Totalitarian and authoritarian regimes experience no such conflict, because they subscribe neither to the civil libertarian nor the democratic values that come into conflict with the value of security. The hard question is, which value is to be preferred when an inevitable clash occurs? One or more of these values must inevitably be compromised in making the tragic choice presented by the ticking bomb case. If we do not torture, we compromise the security and safety of our citizens. If we tolerate torture, but keep it off the books and below the radar screen, we compromise principles of democratic accountability. If we create a legal structure for limiting and controlling torture, we compromise our principled opposition to torture in all circumstances and create a potentially dangerous and expandable situation.

In 1678, the French writer François duc de La Rouchefoucauld put it well when he said, "Hypocrisy is the homage that vice renders to virtue." In this case we have two vices: terrorism and torture. We also have two virtues: civil liberties and democratic accountability (plus, of course, safety). Most civil libertarians I know prefer hypocrisy, precisely because it appears to avoid the conflict between security and civil liberties, but by choosing the way of the hypocrite these civil libertarians compromise the value of democratic accountability. Such is the nature of tragic choices in a complex world. As Bentham put it more than two centuries ago, "Government throughout is but a choice of evils" (Bentham 211). In a democracy, such choices must be made, whenever possible, with openness, democratic accountability, and subject to the rule of law.

Consider another terrible choice of evils that could easily have been presented on September 11, 2001—and may well be presented in the future: a hijacked passenger jet is on a collision course with a densely occupied office building; the only way to prevent the destruction of the building and the killing of its occupants is to shoot down the jet, thereby killing its innocent passengers. This choice now seems easy, since the passengers are certain to die anyway and their somewhat earlier death will save numerous lives. The passenger jet must be shot down. But what if it were only *probable*, not certain, that the jet would crash into the building? Say, for example, we know from cell phone transmissions that passengers are struggling to regain control of the hijacked jet but it is unlikely they will succeed in time. Or say we have no communication with the jet and all we know is that it is off course and heading toward Washington, DC, or some other densely populated city. Under these more questionable circumstances, the question becomes *who* should make this life-and-death choice—a decision that may turn out tragically wrong?

No reasonable person would allocate this decision to a fighter jet pilot who happened to be in the area or to a local airbase commander—unless, of course, there was no time for the matter to be passed up the chain of command to the president or secretary of defense. A decision of this kind should be made at the highest level possible, with visibility and accountability.

Why is this not also true of the decision to torture a ticking bomb terrorist? Why should that choice of evils be relegated to a local policeman, an FBI agent, or a CIA operative—to Jack Bauer—rather than to a judge, the attorney general, or the president? In *24*, sometimes the president authorizes the torture, but he is gradually shrouded in plausible deniability.

There are, of course, important differences between the decision to

shoot down the plane and the decision to torture the ticking bomb terrorist. The former, though tragic, is not likely to be a recurring issue.
There is no slope down which to slip. Moreover the jet to be shot down
is filled with our fellow citizens—people with whom we can identify.
The suspected terrorist we may choose to torture is a "they"—an enemy
with whom we do not identify but with whose potential victims we do
identify. The risk of making the wrong decision, or of overdoing the torture, is far greater, since we do not care as much what happens to "them"
as to "us." (The pilot who would have been responsible for shooting
down the hijacked plane heading from Pennsylvania to D.C. has praised
the passengers who apparently struggled with the hijackers causing the
plane to crash. These brave passengers spared him the dreadful task of
shooting down a plane full of fellow Americans. The stakes are different
when it comes to torturing enemy terrorists.)

Finally, there is something different about torture—even non-lethal
torture—than about a quick death. In addition to the horrible history
associated with torture, there is also the aesthetic of torture. The very
idea of deliberately subjecting a captive human being to excruciating
pain violates our sense of what is acceptable. On a purely rational basis,
it is far worse to shoot a fleeing felon in the back and kill him, yet every
civilized society authorizes the shooting of fleeing felons who pose dangers of committing violent crimes against the policeman or others. In
the United States we execute convicted murderers, despite compelling
evidence of the unfairness and ineffectiveness of capital punishment. Yet
many of us recoil at the prospect of shoving a sterilized needle under the
finger of a suspect who is refusing to divulge information that might prevent multiple deaths. Despite the irrationality of these distinctions, they
are understandable, especially in light of the sordid history of torture.

I disagree with the more passive approaches suggested by some and
believe that in a democracy it is always preferable to decide controversial issues in advance, rather than in the heat of battle.

Even if government officials decline to discuss such issues, academics
have a duty to raise them and submit them to the marketplace of ideas.
So do artists, writers, and the media. There may be danger in open discussion, but there is far greater danger in actions based on secret discussion, or no discussion at all.

These are the issues about which I have tried to begin a reasonable debate in the United States, as I had previously done in Israel. But unlike in Israel, where the debate did take place, in our country its terms were often distorted into a traditional discussion of the pros and cons of torture. Perhaps the most extreme example of this distortion took place at a conference held at John Jay College in New York, to which I was invited to deliver a keynote address about my proposal. The conference began with an emotional speech—replete with candles—delivered by a victim of torture who described how innocent people are tortured to death by brutal regimes around the world. The intended message of this introduction was that torture of the kind experienced by the speaker is bad—as if that were a controversial proposition. It was calculated to make it difficult, if not impossible, to conduct a rational discussion about ways of limiting and regulating the use of non-lethal torture in the context of terrorism prevention. Anyone who expressed any skepticism about simply reiterating a total ban on all torture was seen as the enemy of civilized human rights, even though the total "ban" now in effect has been a license for hypocrisy and pervasive torture with deniability.

Instead of engaging me in a nuanced debate about accountability and choice of evils, critics of my proposal have accused me of "circumventing constitutional prohibitions on torture," giving "thumbs up to torture," "proposing torture for captured terrorist leaders," according U.S. agencies "the right to torture those suspected of withholding information in a terrorist case," and "advocating . . . shoving a sterilized needle under the fingernails of those subjects being interrogated." "Famed Lawyer Backs Use of Torture" read one headline, while another article reported that I urged governments to "put aside the moral issues." One reviewer has even called me "Torquemada Dershowitz," a reference to the notorious torturer of the Inquisition. (No one, however, reminded readers that it was the liberal Jeremy Bentham who made the most powerful utilitarian case for limited torture of convicted criminals to gather information necessary to prevent serious future crime.) Judge Richard Posner of the U.S. Court of Appeals for the Seventh Circuit alleged that I "recommend . . . that suspected terrorists be tortured for information by having needles stuck under their fingernails"—a suggestion that he characterizes as "tinged with sadism" (Tribe).

Let me once again state my actual views on torture, so that no one can any longer feign confusion about where I stand, though I'm certain the "confusion" will persist among some who are determined to argue that I am a disciple of Torquemada. I pose the issue as follows: If torture is, in fact, being used, and/or would, in fact, be used in an actual ticking bomb terrorist case, would it be *normatively* better or worse to have such torture regulated by some kind of warrant, with accountability, record-keeping, standards, and limitations? *This* is an important debate, and *a different one* from the old, abstract Benthamite debate over whether torture can ever be justified. *It* is not so much about the substantive issue of torture, as it is over accountability, visibility, and candor in a democracy that is confronting a choice of evils.

I am against torture as a *normative* matter, and I would like to see its use minimized. I believe that at least moderate forms of non-lethal torture are in *fact* being used by the United States and some of its allies today. I think that if we ever confronted an actual case of imminent mass terrorism that could be prevented by the infliction of torture, we would use torture (even lethal torture) and the public would favor its use.

Whatever option our nation eventually adopts—no torture even to prevent massive terrorism, no torture except with a warrant authorizing non-lethal torture, or no "officially" approved torture but its selective use beneath the radar screen—the choice is ours to make in a democracy. We do have a choice, and we should make it—before low-level operatives make it for us on the basis of a false assumption that we do not really "have a choice."

Regular viewers of *24* are keenly aware of the choice Jack Bauer generally makes. His job is to save innocent lives, not to strike appropriate balances between security and liberty. *That* choice must be made, in a democracy, by the people. *24*—along with other controversial "speech"—helps to inform that choice.

ALAN M. DERSHOWITZ is a Brooklyn native who has been called "the nation's most peripatetic civil liberties lawyer" and one of its "most distinguished defenders of individual rights," "the best-known criminal lawyer in the world," "the top lawyer of last resort," and "America's most public Jewish defender." He is the Felix Frankfurter Professor of Law at Harvard Law School and the author of twenty-seven works of fiction and nonfiction, including six bestsellers. More than a million of his books have been sold worldwide, in numerous languages, and more than a million people have heard him lecture around the world. His most recent nonfiction titles are *Finding Jefferson: A Lost Letter, A Remarkable Discovery*, and *The First Amendment in An Age of Terrorism, Preemption: A Knife That Cuts Both Ways* (2006, Norton), *The Case for Peace: How the Arab-Israeli Conflict Can Be Resolved* (August 2005, Wiley); *Rights From Wrongs: A Secular Theory of the Origins of Rights* (2004, Basic Books), and *The Case for Israel* (2003, Wiley). You can find out more at www.alandershowitz.com.

REFERENCES

Aussaresses, Paul. *The Battle of the Casbah: Terrorism and Counter-Terrorism in Algeria 1955-1957*. NY: Enigma Books, 2002.

Bentham, Jeremy. *The Works of Jeremy Bentham: Published under the Superintendence of His Executor, John Bowring, Volume 4*. Boston: Adamant Media Corporation, 2001.

"Convention against Torture and Other Cruel, Inhumane or Degrading Treatment or Punishment." *Office of the High Commissioner of Human Rights*. 6 Sep. 2007. <http://www.unhchr.ch/html/menu3/b/h_cat39.htm >

Green, Adam. "Normalizing Torture on '24'." *New York Times*, 22 May 2005.

Grey, Barry. "U.S. Oversees Abduction, Torture, Execution of Alleged Terrorists." *Washington Post*, 20 Mar. 2002.

Heymann, Philip B. "Torture Should Not Be Authorized." *Boston Globe*, 16 Feb. 2002.

Langbein, John. *Torture and the Law of Proof*. Chicago: University of Chicago

Press, 1977.

Lewis, Anthony. "Taking Our Liberties." *New York Times,* 9 Mar. 2002.

Maccoy, Alfred W. A *Question of Torture: CIA Interrogation, from the Cold War to the War on Terror.* New York: Metropolitan Books, 2006.

Shister, Gail. "'24' Tamps Down the Torture." *Philadelphia Inquirer,* 16 Feb. 2007.

"Symposium on the Report of the Commission of Inquiry into the Methods of Investigation of the General Security Service Regarding Hostile Terrorist Activity: The Landau Commission Report." *Israeli Law Review.* 23:2–3 (1989).

"The Bojinka Plot." *Wikipedia.* 6 Sep. 2007. <http://en.wikipedia.org/wiki/The_Bojinka_Plot >

Tribe, Laurence H. "CORRESPONDENCE": *New Republic,* 14 Oct. 2002.

Twining, W.L., and P.E. Twining. "Bentham on Torture." *Northern Ireland Legal Quarterly* (1973).

U.S.A. v. Cobb, 1 S.C.R. 587. (2001).

"We Have Ways to Make Them Talk." *The Week.* 6 Sep. 2007. <http://www.theweekmagazine.com/news/articles/news.aspx?ArticleID=225>

Wheeler, Tim. "Congress Adopts Dangerous Terror Bill-FBI Weighs Torture 'Option'." *People's Weekly World Newspaper,* 27 Oct. 2001.

The Reality of Interrogation

ELI LAKE

Jack Bauer knows something that polite society does not: torture works. Whether it's simulating the execution of a terrorist's family, the fear of pain, or the application of pain (either injected or makeshift; a lamp and a live socket will do), every man breaks.

The military and intelligence services would be detaining and interrogating terrorists with or without 24, but in its own way the show has become part of the public debate. Bill Clinton in 2006 said there are exceptions when "of course" torture should be allowed, and then proceeded to give the Jack Bauer example of the ticking bomb. When his wife was asked about this at a debate in New Hampshire in September 2007, she averred, saying it should never be policy. "These hypotheticals are very dangerous," she said. "Because they open a great big hole in what should be an attitude that our country and our president takes toward the appropriate treatment of everyone. And I think it's dangerous to go down this path."

According to many of our cultural elites, torture does not work. There is the problem of the false confession. Plus, how can we as a nation diplomatically criticize torture states, if we ourselves torture? Eventually *ad hoc* torture practices will lead to the tormenting of the innocent, such as in Abu-Ghraib. What the admirers of Jack Bauer do not know, the responsibles tell us, is that 24 is just a television show. The time bomb is almost never actually ticking, often the detained are innocent (and know very little anyway), and establishing trust between the questioner and the questioned is more effective than stress positions and rooms at arctic or boiling temperatures.

It's worth asking, however, what it is that we really know about any of this. The truth is the experts know very little about whether torture even really works, something both sides tend to take for granted. Take for example a study released this year by the National Defense Intelligence Council titled "Educing Information: Interrogation, Science and Art." In his essay in that volume, Robert Coulam, a professor at Simmons College, concluded:

> Whether we like it or not, coercion might be more "effective" than other methods in some circumstances. Unfortunately, much of the current debate in this area proceeds as if we actually knew what those circumstances were. In fact, we do not, beyond anecdotal evidence adduced ad hoc.

Robert Destro, in the foreword of the study, goes further, chiding Hollywood writers for presuming that the tactics of police states can also effectively prevent terrorism:

> The writers craft the script using "extreme" measures because they assume, as our own government has, that police-state tactics studied for defensive purposes can be "reverse engineered" and morphed into cost-effective, "offensive" measures. Though eminently understandable, such reactions are incredibly short-sighted and profoundly unethical. We don't need just any answers, we need good answers. Our health and safety, and our posterity, depend on it.

Further obscuring the matter, actual interrogators are rarely heard from regarding the controversy. Most of the voices in the torture debate are lawyers who raise issues about how the current global war is not waged in the confines of the Geneva Conventions. While former generals have weighed in on the torture debate to bemoan the prospect that a military that tortures its enemies will have its soldiers tortured in turn, the basic question about whether torture works is never addressed head on.

One reason why we don't have anything more to go on than anecdotes is that the best practices for interrogators developed during the Cold War have never been rigorously researched; the prospect is itself grotesque.

Suppose that the National Defense Intelligence Council found that the application of nerve-inflaming injections, a technique explored in 24, was very effective at educing information from suspected terrorists. And over time, suppose that a division of the CIA perfected these drugs and their application. Given the time, energy, and money spent on the project, would we not risk turning a temporary practice—the use of nerve-inflaming injection in moments of national emergency—into a permanent one? F. A. Hayek observed more than sixty years ago that no government bureaucracy will ever submit a budget that justifies itself out of existence; this is doubly true for a secret bureaucracy. Once a bureaucracy starts perfecting torture there is a risk it will never stop.

I have no special insights into what specific kinds of torture work. Some forms must work or few governments would bother with the grim practice. I have interviewed terrorists who have been broken by torture and who have confessed. I have also spent time in interrogation facilities in Iraq, a country whose counterterrorism forces contend every day with the kind of perpetual terror that comes close to the nightmarish world of 24. I also have spoken to enough intelligence officers on the inside to know that the public debate does not reflect the reality of the interrogation world.

So let's look at the real world of interrogation.

The first thought you have when you see a man in a blindfold with his arms tied behind his back is that he looks like a hostage . . . just as a man in a ski mask looks like a bank robber and a man wearing a hood looks like he is about to be executed.

In Iraq, the translators for the army wear ski masks, the ethnic cleansers (the terrorists) look and talk like civilians, and suspected hostage takers and executioners are bound and blindfolded when Iraqi and American forces catch them.

On May 4, 2007, inside the headquarters for Lt. Colonel Rahim al-Bakri's Iraqi Army battalion, Camp Honor, the man's binds and fold are loosened so a soldier can allow him to sip water. Before the session began he was given a cursory medical exam and photographed to protect the prisoner from mistreatment and to protect the interrogators from false charges, a procedure that is the result in part of the vigilance of U.S. Army Major Christopher Norrie's Military Transition Team, a sixteen-man unit that fights alongside Colonel Rahim's men every day in the east Mansour neighborhood of Baghdad. A big part of what Major Norrie and Colonel Rahim do is try to catch terrorists, but they know that without the trust of the residents their fight is futile.

The interrogator, Captain Amjed, is no Jack Bauer. He rarely raises his voice. The suspect, named Dheyaa, is surrounded by Iraqi soldiers, an American officer, a translator, and me. The suspect sits Indian-style against the wall of a hallway, outside the door of one of the interrogation rooms. His voice at times cracks as he answers a barrage of questions about his whereabouts, the numbers in his cell phone, and his affiliation with al-Qaeda.

Colonel Rahim touted Dheyaa, some twelve hours earlier on May 4, as the "Prince of Hatin." In the Baghdad street vernacular, a prince is a man who has beheaded at least ten people, and Hatin is a neighborhood in the battalion's sector, where Mr. Rahim's soldiers have set up traffic checkpoints and an ambush site near its main market. The soldiers who man the ambush point — no more than three concrete slabs atop a small mound of wire caged earth, or what the military call a "hesco barrier" — use a nearby doctor's office as a makeshift barracks. Fearing reprisals from al-Qaeda, the doctors have fled.

For Colonel Rahim, the apprehension of the suspected prince was a welcome dose of good news on a relatively bad weekend. On May 3, terrorists in nearby Ahmariya kidnapped the younger brother of one of his lieutenants at a bank. The incident sparked a series of consultations with the American military transition team advising his battalion and the worry that they would have to choose between the life of one of his officers and the life of the officer's younger brother. It turned out the terrorists only wanted Lieutenant Mustapha to give them cash and make a video denouncing and apologizing for his decision to join the Iraqi Army. Eventually Mustapha was reunited with his brother, but only after he risked a dangerous encounter with the kidnappers and his batallion sweated out a weekend of waiting.

A member of Iraq's parliament tipped off Colonel Rahim that a high-ranking terrorist was using a small nearby flat as a safe house. Dheyaa fit the description of the high-ranking terrorist. Since I also knew the member of the Iraqi parliament, Colonel Rahim offered to let me sit in on the detention.

When I arrive, it looks like the prince has already been broken. "Are you scared?" Captain Amjed asks him.

"I hope to Allah that you will not execute me. I am just trying to run my business," Dheyaa replies. The suspect repeats that he is a simple worker, a clerk at the Treasury Ministry.

(Later on, Captain Amjed said matter-of-factly that almost every terrorist calls out to Allah to proclaim his innocence when he is caught.)

Nonetheless, some details emerge that make me doubt that Dheyaa is really a prince. Crumpled up in his breast pocket is a little over three dollars worth of Dinars. Terror princes in Baghdad not only behead their victims, they also finance operations and pay off locals to plant improvised explosives. It seems unlikely that a man of this stature would have barely enough money for a week's groceries.

While Dheyaa is not touched, he is indirectly threatened. Captain Amjed says he will send him to a facility "where they will not treat [him] like a human being."

Another soldier chimes in and says that he could fix him some egg-plant and a Pepsi, if only he admitted to being who they thought he was.

When this tactic fails, the soldiers try the expray test, a test using a chemical spray that purports to detect the residue of explosives. Captain Amjed tries his best to extract a confession from Dheyaa before he sprays the suspect's palm. After the test comes up positive for TNT, Captain Amjed crows that he now has evidence that the detainee is a prince.

Faced with the results, Dheyaa points to the ceiling and cries out, "Allah, you know better. Allah, you know better."

But he does not confess to being the prince.

You couldn't tell from the interrogation, but Captain Amjed had his doubts about the suspect all along. "I didn't think he was the prince when he came willingly to the door at the raid," he said later. The problem was that Colonel Rahim had received a tip from a member of parliament whose information had been reliable in the past. Intelligence is never a certainty and Captain Amjed had to make sure.

It turns out that the expray test often mistakes the residue of cigarette smoke for TNT. An American intelligence officer, Lieutenant Ellison, tells Major Norrie later that these tests would not be accepted in the United States. Captain Amjed decides to tell Colonel Rahim that their prince is really a pauper.

At first Colonel Rahim seems incredulous. He asks about the expray test, which he was told earlier had yielded a positive match. But he agrees to speak with his original source, who backs away from the story under scrutiny. "If this is not the man, then why did you tell us he was?" the colonel says on the phone. The member of parliament says that, in retrospect, the prince might have been Dheyaa's brother.

With the case against the prince in shambles, Colonel Rahim instructs his soldiers to let him go.

Major Norrie is pleased. "You are brave enough and strong enough to make the right decision," he says.

"I cannot upset the people here," Colonel Rahim replies.

Major Norrie recommends Colonel Rahim invite Dheyaa to his office and apologize.

Inside the colonel's modest office, which also serves as a bedroom and kitchen, Colonel Rahim wastes no time with Dheyaa, who looks exhausted and bewildered after nearly two hours of questioning. "We are sorry. The information we got about you said you were a very dangerous man. We talked to the guy who gave us this and we know it is false," Colonel Rahim says.

Dheyaa begins to cry.

Colonel Rahim continues: "Saddam is gone now. We don't build an army on fear now. We heard you were the prince, but the information was wrong. You are one of my brothers." Colonel Rahim gives Dheyaa his personal cell phone number and both men grip each other in a tight hug. Colonel Rahim kisses his target from the morning on both cheeks. The officer and the treasury clerk, the interrogator and the interogatee, go out to dinner.

On the way from Camp Honor, Major Norrie beams. "That was a

counterterrorism win for us," he says. "A counterterrorism win."

Major Norrie's victory does not make sense in the world of counterterrorism depicted in *24*. In that world, Iraq in a sense has already failed, as have America's other efforts overseas to address the jihad's source of oxygen, the suffocation of political and economic opportunity abroad. The show exists in an America whose national security policy has failed, leaving the CTU as the last line of desperate defense against a series of disasters.

For Iraq to work, it must emerge from its current war against terrorist saboteurs with a military, police, and government that has earned the trust of Iraqis. All I know, having been there in the interrogation room, is that eliminating the all-too-common torture in that country is the best hope we have to avoid its practice here at home.

ELI LAKE is a senior reporter for the *New York Sun*. Before that he was the chief diplomatic correspondent for United Press International. Mr. Lake's work has appeared in the *Washington Post*, the *Los Angeles Times*, the *New Republic*, the *Weekly Standard*, the *National Review*, and the *Washington Times*.

In his reporting he has traveled to all five continents and all three members of the Axis of Evil. In 2005 and 2006, Mr. Lake lived and reported for a year from Cairo for the *New York Sun*.

REFERENCES

CNN.com. "Clinton shifts position on torture policy." 27 September 2007. <http://politicalticker.blogs.cnn.com/2007/09/27/clinton-flip-flops-on-torture-policy/>

National Defense Intelligence College (U.S.). "Educing Information: Interrogation, Science and Art: Foundations for the Future." <www.fas.org/irp/dni/educing.pdf>

Jack (Bauer) and the Beanstalk

The Power of Imagination in Understanding the Terrorist Mind

DAVEED GARTENSTEIN-ROSS AND KYLE DABRUZZI

I think one of the reasons *24* is popular is it's fun to make fun of. I mean, how many times can we be shocked to learn that the Counter Terrorism Unit is pretty much a hotbed of terrorist agents?

—Dave Barry

Before 9/11, the only person at high levels of government who suspected that al-Qaeda might use airplanes as guided missiles was counterterrorism czar Richard Clarke. Did his suspicions come from a detailed knowledge of intelligence reports or a nuanced reading of other classified information? No. His line of thinking was inspired by a Tom Clancy novel.

The leaps of imagination that fiction allows can sometimes provide insight into terrorist thought that standard intelligence analysis does not. Although certain terrorist tactics and targets consistently recur, terrorism is at heart a creative enterprise: the best and most lethal terrorists are those who can transform fertile and vicious imaginations into reality. Yet often the chattering class has trouble understanding the role imag-

133

ination plays in terrorist plots—and the corresponding role of imagination in defeating terrorism. Witness the voluminous commentary dismissing 24 plots as mere fairy tales. One blogger described the show as "fantasy and hi-tech silliness and soap-opera-ish nonsense, and just over-all ridiculous on so many levels" (*The Damage in My Face* 3-14-07). While such criticisms aren't completely baseless, they fail to credit the potential utility of the creative processes that go into the show.

To be sure, a season of 24 has more twists and turns than Sunset Boulevard. Some aspects of the plot are exaggerated or accelerated for dramatic effect. The show depicts the United States as a quasi banana republic where factions actively plot against the president—often with great success, as evidenced by the fact that 24 has seen seven different presidents in its six seasons. (In reality, plotting factions among the unelected bureaucracy and president's men usually attain less clear-cut victories. Presidents are not toppled, but midlevel officials are cashiered.) Equally unrealistic if less dramatic is Jack Bauer's head-scratching ability to reach any location in Los Angeles in five minutes by car. He appears to be the only man alive who can drive through L.A. faster than a plane can fly over it. Then there is Jack's similarly far-fetched ability to survive torture, explosions, and gunshots. As Ramon Salazar observed in season three, "The man has more lives than a cat" (3-9).

But beyond Jack's impressive shot-to-kill ratio and the show's penchant for high-level conspiracies, the skepticism displayed toward 24 reflects a lack of imagination concerning terrorist machinations. This lack of imagination is mirrored in other areas of the public understanding of terrorism. When Khalid Sheikh Mohammed confessed before the Combatant Status Review Tribunal at the Guantanamo Bay detention facility to involvement in thirty-one separate terrorist plots, the primary public reaction was deep skepticism. Many people simply refused to believe that one man could be involved in so much mischief. But in Mohammed's case, these doubts actually ran counter to the bulk of the evidence: a good deal of his terrorist involvement had been in the public record even before the confession.

———

Just as there was more evidence to Mohammed's nefarious activities than the public's skepticism suggested, there is also more resemblance between 24's terrorist plots and our enemies' actual plans than initially meets the eye.

In season one, two cooperating terrorist groups plotted to assassinate David Palmer, a candidate for the Democratic presidential nomination. In season five, terrorists tried to assassinate Russian president Yuri Suvarov by attacking his motorcade during a visit to the United States. Similarly, Islamic terror groups have plotted the assassination of prominent international figures, high-ranking U.S. officials, and former officials. In the mid-1990s, Khalid Sheikh Mohammed himself plotted to assassinate then-president Bill Clinton and Pope John Paul II during their visits to the Philippines (Sageman 164). He also plotted to kill former president Jimmy Carter ("31 Plots"). American citizen Ahmed Omar Abu Ali—former valedictorian of the Islamic Saudi Academy in Alexandria, Virginia—was recently charged with planning to assassinate President George W. Bush by either shooting him on the street or detonating a car bomb near him (*United States v. Ahmed Omar Abu Ali*). And terrorists have tried to kill Dick Cheney, Paul Wolfowitz, and other American officials during their travels overseas (Wafa, Ignatius).

Americans have not been the only government officials targeted. Islamic terrorists have tried to kill Pakistani president Pervez Musharraf and Afghan president Hamid Karzai on multiple occasions ("A Look at Assassination Attempts," "UN 'Outraged'"), plotted to kill Benazir Bhutto when she led Pakistan (Burke), and have made attempts on many other foreign officials. These attempts often succeed, as the high mortality rate among Afghan and Iraqi politicians can attest. Two days before 9/11, two suicide bombers disguised as journalists killed Ahmad Shah Massoud, the leader of the Northern Alliance that challenged the Taliban's dominance in Afghanistan (Rashid).

————

Another terrorist device on *24* that aligns with actual terrorist thinking is the desire to strike with weapons of mass destruction. Season two's storyline centered on a terrorist faction called Second Wave that wanted to detonate an airborne nuclear weapon over Los Angeles. Season six focused on the plans of Islamic terrorists led by Abu Fayed, who wanted to detonate five nuclear bombs, each in a different American city.

Similarly, there can be little doubt that al-Qaeda is fervently pursuing nuclear capability. The terrorist group entered the market for nuclear weapons in the early 1990s when Osama bin Laden was in Sudan. Former al-Qaeda operative Jamal al-Fadl has described an attempt to buy a uranium cylinder from a former Sudanese government minister in 1993-1994. Fortunately, al-Qaeda ruefully learned that the cylinder contained only radioactive hospital waste. The terror network had been scammed.

Al-Qaeda was also duped in at least one other attempted purchase of weapons-grade uranium, but has since become increasingly sophisticated in its efforts. In his book *At the Center of the Storm*, former CIA director George Tenet reveals that in 2002-2003, senior al-Qaeda leaders in Saudi Arabia were negotiating for the purchase of Russian nuclear devices. When these negotiations were relayed to senior al-Qaeda leader Saif al-Adl, Tenet writes that al-Adl replied that no price was too high for such weapons, but cautioned "that al-Qai'da had been stung by scams in the past and that Pakistani specialists should be brought to Saudi Arabia to inspect the merchandise prior to purchase" (Tenet 272). Al-Qaeda's readiness to bring Pakistani specialists into the negotiations to ensure the devices' reliability is indicative of their determination to get it right this time.

Beyond nuclear weapons, 24's terrorist plots have also included biological and chemical weapons. Season three's villains wanted to unleash the deadly Cordilla virus on Los Angeles, and in season five twenty canisters of Sentox VX1 nerve gas were deployed at various targets around the city. Terrorists have actually carried out chemical and biological attacks in the past, and their interest in these weapons continues.

The clearest example of a biological attack in the U.S. was the anthrax scare that occurred just after 9/11. Senators Tom Daschle and Patrick Leahy, as well as various news agencies, were targeted by letters containing spores of the bacterial disease. Thankfully, only five people died as a result—and most analysts believe the anthrax attacks were not connected to Islamic terror.

Tokyo experienced a horrific chemical attack in 1995 when members of the Aum Shinrikyo cult released Sarin nerve gas in the city's subways. Fifteen stations were affected, and nearly a thousand people had to be hospitalized. Twelve died.

Al-Qaeda has shown a clear interest in biological and chemical weapons. It has eyed a variety of delivery systems, ranging from crop dusters to the *mubtakkar*, a device highlighted in Ron Suskind's *The One Percent Doctrine* that was intended to distribute deadly hydrogen-cyanide gas. Millennium bomber Ahmed Ressam acknowledged in court testimony that al-Qaeda had conducted gruesome experiments on dogs by sticking them in boxes, then gassing them or injecting them with cyanide. Moreover, recent events are indicative of al-Qaeda's willingness to put chemical weapons to use, as al-Qaeda in Iraq has employed chlorine gas in a number of attacks since February 2007.

Al-Qaeda obtained theological permission to use weapons of mass destruction in May 2003, when Saudi cleric Nasir bin Hamid al-Fahd published "A Treatise on the Legal Status of Using Weapons of Mass Destruction Against Infidels," a justification for WMD terrorism against the United States. This is no mere flight of fancy, but a legitimate threat.

––––

A further parallel between *24*'s terrorist plots and those of real-life terrorists is the use of hostage taking as a tool of coercion. *24*'s terrorists have taken hostages in an effort to make Jack, CTU, or the U.S. government accede to their demands. Of course, more often than not, *24*'s recipe for dealing with hostage taking is a timely intervention by Jack Bauer, complemented by a dollop of ass-kicking.

In season one, Teri and Kim Bauer were taken hostage in a bid to force Jack to cooperate in a plot to assassinate David Palmer. Even after the terrorists who initially captured the two women were defeated, Kim was taken hostage a second time. In season four, the first subplot involved terrorists taking defense secretary James Heller and his daughter hostage. Heller was placed before a camera in an orange jumpsuit reminiscent of the gruesome Nicholas Berg execution tape, and put on trial for "war crimes." Thankfully, before Heller could be executed, Jack Bauer took out the twenty-plus terrorists surrounding the building and freed him.

In season five, Russian separatist leader Anton Beresch took hostages in California's Ontario International Airport, demanding that the U.S. and Russia call off the antiterrorism accord they were on the verge of signing. Although one hostage was executed before a camera, Jack saved the day before further blood was spilled.

Real-life terrorists have also shown an affinity for taking hostages, and have used this tactic in an attempt to coerce or intimidate various governments. Often their demands are for a prisoner exchange, or the removal of troops from Iraq or other Muslim countries. The al-Qaeda manual

Declaration of Jihad Against the Country's Tyrants includes instructions for the interrogation of hostages, stating that it is permissible to "strike the non-believer who has no covenant until he reveals the news, information, and secrets of his people" (Gunaratna 101). Further, the manual allows "the killing of a hostage if he insists on withholding information from Muslims," and "the exchange of hostages for money, services, expertise, and secrets of the enemy's army, plans, and numbers" (Gunaratna 101). Clearly, *24* does not exaggerate the use of hostage taking as a terrorist tactic.

———

Terrorists' use of moles in *24* is also echoed in real life—although the real-life echoes are far dimmer than *24*, where CTU is full of traitors, knaves, and radicals. In season one, Ira Gaines—who led the group that initially kidnapped Teri and Kim Bauer—made use of CTU analyst Jamey Farrell, whose loyalty he managed to purchase. In season two Marie Warner, an ally of arch-terrorist Syed Ali, aided Ali from within her father's business. And season four's plotters were assisted by Marianne Taylor, who was working for CTU Los Angeles.

But the classic mole in *24* is without question Nina Myers, former second-in-command at CTU Los Angeles. She was involved in Victor Drazen's plot to kill David Palmer in season one, provided Joseph Wald's Patriots with CTU's schematics and security protocols before they bombed it in season two, and tried to buy the Cordilla virus in season three.

In reality, al-Qaeda has never placed a high-level mole inside the U.S. government, at least as far as we know. The terrorist group would have to overcome a number of cultural and religious barriers to accomplish that. But al-Qaeda has been able to find lower-level moles in the United States—and some high-level allies in the Middle East.

Al-Qaeda's U.S. moles include Ali Mohamed (a U.S. Army sergeant assigned to a Special Forces unit at Fort Bragg, North Carolina, before he became a conspirator in the 1998 East African embassy bombing plot) and National Guardsman Ryan Anderson. Anderson, a tank crewman in the 81st Armored Brigade who converted to Islam, was convicted in 2004 of attempting to aid the enemy. In a meeting with investigators posing as al-Qaeda members, Anderson provided sketches of the M1A1 tank and described its weaknesses. At one point, he told undercover military personnel, "I wish to desert from the U.S. Army. I wish to defect from the United States. I wish to join al-Qaeda, train its members and conduct terrorist attacks" (Mitchell).

Outside the U.S., our terrorist enemies have found far more powerful allies in official circles. Abdallah bin Khalid al-Thani, a member of the Qatari royal family, helped Khalid Sheikh Mohammed escape when the FBI was on the verge of arresting him in Doha in 1996. American intelligence officials have revealed that al-Thani tipped off Mohammed—and that bin Laden himself visited al-Thani in Qatar between 1996 and 2000. A former CIA official told ABC News that others in the Qatari royal family also sympathized with al-Qaeda, and provided members of the terrorist group with safe haven.

In Yemen, former interior minister Hussein Arab seemingly aided alleged mastermind Abd al-Rahim al-Nashiri in the USS *Cole* bombing. In early 2000, Arab penned an official letter telling security services to give safe passage to Sheik Mohammed Omar al-Harazi (one of al-Nashiri's aliases) "without being searched or intercepted. All security forces are instructed to cooperate with him and facilitate his missions" (Watkins). After this document became known publicly, political analyst Mohammed al-Sabri stated that it "confirms that there is a breach in the Yemeni security system. This system has been infiltrated for a long time by terrorist elements" (Watkins).

———

Although *24*'s portrayal of terrorist motivations is far from brilliant, this is another area where the show's terrorists track those we encounter in the real world. The terrorists of *24* have had several opportunities to explain their war against the West. When secretary of defense James Heller was held captive in season four and put on trial for "war crimes," one of the terrorist leaders read from their "indictment":

> Since the true extent of your evil legacy is immeasurable, we have done our best to document it, those acts which have been witnessed directly by the chosen followers. Under your orders, the death squads of America continue their imperialistic crusade against the true believers and pure followers. . . . There is no place in this world where your evil has not scoured the land of the true word. Your imperialist legacy has devoured the lives of

the innocent. . . . We hold you responsible for blasphemy, for desecrating holy lands and shrines, and for spilling the blood of our brothers. (4-6)

Later that season, arch-terrorist Habib Marwan echoed these sentiments in a pre-recorded video that turned out to be an embarrassingly premature celebration of victory:

People of America, you wake up today to a different world. One of your own nuclear weapons has been used against you. It will be days or weeks before you can measure the damage we have caused. . . . Unless you renounce your policies of imperialism and interventionist activities, this attack will be followed by another and another after that. (4-20)

Osama bin Laden similarly painted a picture of an arrogant, over-reaching United States in two separate declarations of war that he issued in 1996 and 1998. Bin Laden outlined three primary grievances in his 1996 declaration, all of which relate to the U.S. role in the Middle East: the UN-sponsored sanctions against Iraq, American troop presence in Saudi Arabia, and U.S. support for Israel. Similar to the contention of 24's terrorists that "[t]here is no place in this world where your evil has not scoured the land of the true word," bin Laden thunders:

It is no secret to you, my brothers, that the people of Islam have been afflicted with oppression, hostility, and injustice by the Judeo-Christian alliance and its supporters. . . . Your blood has been spilt in Palestine and Iraq, and the horrific image of the massacre in Qana in Lebanon is still fresh in people's minds. The massacres that have taken place in Tajikistan, Burma, Kashmir, Assam, the Philippines, Fatani, Ogaden, Somalia, Eritrea, Chechnya, and Bosnia-Herzegovina send shivers down our spines and stir up our passions. All this has happened before the eyes and ears of the world, but the blatant imperial arrogance of America, under the cover of the immoral United Nations, has prevented the dispossessed from arming themselves. (Lawrence 25)

Bin Laden struck similar notes in his 1998 declaration of war, and his deputy Ayman al-Zawahiri has likewise painted a picture of an imperialistic, bloodthirsty United States in his voluminous writings and speeches. Bin Laden and Zawahiri go into far more depth in their critiques of the United States and the West than do the terrorists of *24*: while *24*'s producers are not oblivious to the grievances of today's terrorists, the show does not provide a full picture of the various factors that make many Muslims believe that their religion is under attack.

Moreover, the terrorism with which we are locked in mortal combat today is not merely political: it is unique precisely because of our enemies' theological worldview and motivations. While this is one of the most difficult aspects of the terrorist mindset to accurately portray—it treads on an admittedly sensitive subject matter—*24* makes little attempt to depict the theological lens through which Islamic terrorists view the world, aside from such instances as Marie Warner's rather lame declaration of "*Allahu akbar!*" ("God is great!") in season two.

The show does, however, offer an interesting depiction of an increasingly problematic trend in the war on terror: the threat of homegrown terrorism, Westerners who feel compelled to take up arms against the societies in which they were raised. In an excellent *New Yorker* profile of al-Qaeda spokesman Adam Gadahn (who grew up on a goat farm in Southern California), Raffi Khatchadourian notes that "because of their cultural literacy, and because of the mobility that their citizenship provides," homegrowns "are potentially the most dangerous of terrorists." One of season two's terrorist conspirators was a homegrown terrorist, American-born Marie Warner.

Most radicalized Westerners view their former lives as decadent, full of ignorance and hypocrisy—and come to exhibit a disregard for non-Muslim friends and family members. According to Marie Warner's father, her mother passed away while she was attending college in London. Soon after that, Marie disappeared. Although the details of what transpired during this period are hazy, Marie later tried to explain her transformation to her sister Kate: "I opened my eyes. That's what happened to me. I was pathetic, just like you, until I met Syed [Ali], until I saw the lies and hypocrisy of my life, of this country, of people like Dad who help the government. . . . Do you have any idea what kind of suffering they cause around the world?" (2-14). Similar to other radicalized Westerners' views of their past lives, Warner saw hers as ignorant and compromised, unthinkingly contributing to the world's woes.

Warner also displayed nothing but scorn for her non-Muslim family members. When Jack Bauer needed Warner to divulge information about the location of a nuclear bomb in the Los Angeles area, he tried having her sister Kate speak with her. But Marie, unfazed by Kate's appeals, stared unblinkingly into her eyes and said, "I'm going to help you stop being part of the problem. I killed Reza [her fiancé] and I loved him. Why would I care about you and Dad?" (2-14).

While Marie Warner's disregard for the people who raised her shocked her sister, it is a disregard shared by other radicalized Westerners. In one video interview, al-Qaeda spokesman Adam Gadahn declared that a Muslim's loyalty "is to Allah, his Messenger, his religion, and his fellow believers before anyone and anything else" (FBI). If this allegiance conflicts with a Muslim's nation or family, Gadahn contends that the Muslim must choose his faith. As an example, he says that in Muhammad's time, "even if they were their fathers or their sons, or their brothers, or their kindred or their clan . . . some of the early Muslims fought and killed their closest relatives during battle" (Khatchadourian).

Indeed, in his profile of Gadahn, Khatchadourian notes that "some of Gadahn's most pointed rhetoric as an Al Qaeda operative" appears directed at his family. Gadahn's father Phil, while a nominal Christian, had a New Age religious sensibility: his theological views seemed to shift with his needs of the moment. Khatchadourian suggests that some of Gadahn's public statements are rebukes of his father:

> "The way to paradise is not a multi-lane highway," Gadahn declares in "An Invitation to Islam," and one can't help but think that he has in mind his father's pliant spirituality. Gadahn admonishes those who embraced, "without hesitation, every obscure and foreign religion, philosophy, and ideology," or who searched for happiness in a "cultist-style withdrawal from the world." In the video's final moments, Gadahn turns to the subject of family, and his message is chilling. "Allah warns the parents, siblings, offspring, and other relatives of the Muslim that their relation to him will be of no use

to them on the day of judgment, if they have not themselves died as true believers," he says. "So don't be complacent, or let the Devil deceive you into thinking that your connections will intercede for you on that terrible day."

24's depiction of the motivations and worldview of its villains is not one of its great strengths, but neither is it unrealistic. Certainly it does not diminish from the critical act of imagination that lies at the heart of 24, and that can provide insight into terrorist plots and machinations.

———

But the importance of imagination to understanding the terrorist mind should not make us lose sight of the fundamental distinction between fact and fiction. For some public sphere "analysts," the difference between the two is unfortunately blurred. Paul Williams, who frequently peddles his theories on sensationalistic Web site WorldNetDaily, has argued for years that bin Laden has smuggled six or seven nuclear weapons into the United States through the Mexican border, and will soon detonate them simultaneously in a horrific "American Hiroshima" (Williams, 2005; Williams, 2006). Williams's belief in this scenario has not wavered despite his unfortunate statement to NewsMax.com in 2004 that he had "no doubt" that bin Laden and al-Qaeda would mount a nuclear attack on U.S. soil before 2005 (Stogel).

Williams's theory would be horrifying if true—and we fully agree that the U.S. government should do everything in its power to prevent a nuclear nightmare on American soil. But does bin Laden *really* have nuclear weapons in the United States? Fortunately, Williams's facts are far less accurate than Jack Bauer's gunshots.

The major source in Williams's reporting is a Pakistani journalist named Hamid Mir, who has become a jihadist favorite because of his credulity and willingness to report low-level jihadi campfire talk as undisputed fact. (He is also a jihadist favorite because of his sympathy with their cause. Mir has described jihad as "the greatest defender of human rights" ["Media Aid"]. When Pakistan's government attempted to arrest Osama bin Laden in 1998, following the bin Laden–orchestrated bombings of U.S. embassies in Kenya and Tanzania, Mir's criticisms were sharp: "Had the raids been successful, the government would have won a new medal. This is a unique medal of the world. It is called the 'Medal for selling a mujahid [holy warrior].' America may declare Usama Bin Ladin a terrorist but common Muslims consider him a mujahid" ["Media Aid"].)

Another prominent source in Williams's book *Dunces of Doomsday* is Ryan Mauro, a community college student in New Jersey. In the chapter devoted to the "American Hiroshima" threat, Mauro is cited three times out of forty-four footnotes. And when one reads the articles by Mauro that were cited, they turn out to be interviews of Williams himself.

The least that can be said is that 24's intelligence analysts are far more thorough than Williams. When the nuclear terrorist plot in season two is unveiled, the NSA staffer charged with briefing the president notes:

> What I'm about to tell you, Mr. President, is triple sourced. And while crucial details are still unknown, we believe this intel to have extremely high credibility. . . . There is a nuclear device under terrorist control that's on U.S. soil. . . . It gets worse. This bomb is going to go off today. . . . When we grabbed [Jason] Park, we tried to extract everything we could out of him. About fifteen minutes ago, he broke and confessed that for the last two years, [Mahmud Rashed] Faheen has been preparing for today's attack on Los Angeles. (2-1)

This statement produced looks of pure panic on the faces of the president and his top advisors. In contrast, if Williams had the chance to brief the president on his information, he would likely be laughed out of the room—even in the fantastical universe of *24*.

———

As the 9/11 Commission noted, the terrorists' success on September 11, 2001, was as much a failure of imagination as it was a failure of intelligence. In addition to entertaining us, shows like *24* can help us envision future terrorist plots.

Not all of the terrorist schemes in *24* are original; many in fact mimic plans that have already been conjured. But this too is consonant with the way terrorists operate. Even the 9/11 plot was derivative. When the

Algeria-based Armed Islamic Group hijacked Air France Flight 8969 in late 1994, the hijackers demanded twenty-seven tons of jet fuel after touching down in Marseille—far more than they would have needed to reach their destination of Paris. After an investigation of the GIA turned up a drawing of an exploding Eiffel Tower, investigators suspected that the hijackers may have "intended to crash the fuel-heavy jet into France's icon" (Bernton). And when terrorist mastermind Ramzi Yousef's right-hand man, Abdul Hakim Murad, was captured by authorities in the Philippines, he told them about plans "to hijack a commercial plane and ram it into the CIA headquarters in Langley, Virginia, and also the Pentagon" (Ressa).

Like Tom Clancy's novels, 24 can help us envision plots that our terrorist enemies may devise—and can provide a dramatization of how these plots might come to fruition, and what the consequences could be. The terrorist plots in 24 can help myopic analysts and officials think beyond their stock paradigms for conceptualizing terrorism.

Will terrorists try to use water-borne improvised explosive devices to attack cruise liners packed with vacationing couples and college spring-breakers? What about spreading chemical agents using the guise of a wildfire? Or what about crashing eighteen-wheelers full of gasoline on major highways during rush hour? Our enemies may not reject such possibilities out of hand. And neither does 24.

Shows like 24 are clearly not fully reflective of reality, but the knee-jerk tendency to brush off the show in its entirety is indicative of a public that has neither learned to appreciate the terrorists' creativity, nor their full destructive potential.

DAVEED GARTENSTEIN-ROSS is the vice president of research at the Foundation for Defense of Democracies and the author of *My Year Inside Radical Islam.*

KYLE DABRUZZI is a summer fellow at the Foundation for Defense of Democracies.

REFERENCES

"31 Plots Listed in Khalid Sheikh Mohammed's Confession." Associated Press, 15 Mar. 2007. <http://www.iht.com/articles/ap/2007/03/16/america/NA-GEN-US-Terrorist-Confession-List.php>

"A Look at Assassination Attempts on Pakistan's President, Gen. Pervez Musharraf." Associated Press, 6 Jul. 2007. <http://www.pr-inside.com/a-look-at-assassination-attempts-on-r166244.htm>

Bernton, Hal, et al. "The Terrorist Tracker." *Seattle Times*, 23 Jun. 2002.

Burke, Jason. "Architect of New York's Day of Terror." *The Observer*, 2 Mar. 2003.

Federal Bureau of Investigation. "Text Transcript of Video Clip Interview with 'Azzam the American.'" No date given (last visited 25 Aug. 2007). <http://www.fbi.gov/terrorinfo/counterrorism/azzam/transcript103004.htm>

Gunaratna, Rohan. *Inside Al-Qaeda: Global Network of Terror.* New York: Berkley Books, 2003.

Ignatius, David. "Volley of Rockets Shatters a Life and Images of Stability." *Washington Post*, 27 Oct. 2003.

Khatchadourian, Raffi. "Azzam the American: The Making of an Al Qaeda Homegrown." *New Yorker.* 22 Jan. 2007.

Lawrence, Bruce. *Messages to the World: The Statements of Osama bin Laden.* London: Verso, 2005.

"Media Aid: Profile of Leading Pakistani Commentator Hamid Mir, U.S. Critic." *Open Source Center Media Aid in English.* 8 Jun. 2006.

Mitchell, Melanthia. "'Net Sleuth' Tells Court of Hunt That Snared Guardsman." *USA Today.* 13 May 2004. <http://www.usatoday.com/news/nation/2004-05-13-netsleuth_x.htm>

Rashid, Ahmed. "Afghanistan Resistance Leader Feared Dead in Blast." *The Telegraph*, 11 Sep. 2001.

Ressa, Maria. "U.S. Warned in 1995 of Plot to Hijack Planes, Attack
Buildings." CNN.com. 18 Sep. 2001. <http://archives.cnn.com/2001/US/
09/18/inv.hijacking.philippines/index.html>

Sageman, Marc. *Understanding Terror Networks.* Philadelphia: University of
Pennsylvania Press, 2004.

Stogel, Stewart. "Bin Laden's Goal: Kill 4 Million Americans." *NewsMax.* 14 Jul.
2004. <http://www.newsmax.com/archives/articles/2004/7/14/215350.shtml>

Tenet, George. *At the Center of the Storm: My Years at the CIA.* New York:
HarperCollins Publishers, 2007.

"UN 'Outraged' After Assassination Attempt on Karzai." Associated Press, 10
Jun. 2007. <http://www.iht.com/articles/ap/2007/06/11/asia/AS-GEN-
Afghan-Violence.php>

United States v. Ahmed Omar Abu Ali, No. 1:05CR53, Indictment (E.D. Va. Feb.
3, 2005).

Wafa, Abdul Waheed. "Cheney Unhurt After Bombing in Afghanistan." *New
York Times,* 24 Feb. 2007.

Watkins, Eric. "Yemen's Innovative Approach to the War on Terror."
Jamestown Foundation Terrorism Monitor. 24 Feb. 2005.
<http://jamestown.org/terrorism/news/article.php?articleid=2369320>

"What Would Jack Bauer Do?" *The Damage in My Face,* 14 Mar. 2007.
<http://thedamageinmyface.blogspot.com/2007/03/what-would-jack-bauer-
do.html>

Williams, Paul. *The Al Qaeda Connection: International Terrorism, Organized
Crime, and the Coming Apocalypse.* Amherst, New York: Prometheus Books,
2005.

_____. *The Dunces of Doomsday: 10 Blunders that Gave Rise to Radical
Islam, Terrorist Regimes, and the Threat of an American Hiroshima.* Nashville,
Tennessee: WND Books, 2006.

Hail to the Chief

KRISTINE KATHRYN RUSCH

A s I write this essay, season six of 24 has just started with its characteristic bang (or, in this case, bangs). Much as I love the plotting, the cliffhangers, and the changes in the life of Jack Bauer
and friends, what I love most about season six is something that has so
far gone unremarked in all the reviews.

Wayne Palmer has just been elected president of the United States—
the second African-American president of the United States.

Now, the real United States has never had a first African-American
president, let alone a second one. In fact, we have never had a Latino
president, an Asian-American president, or a female president. Every
president we've had has been white, male, and (theoretically) a practicing Christian.

We patted ourselves on the back in 1960 because we elected a
Catholic (see? No prejudice here), and we did so again when Al Gore
nominated a practicing Jew as his running mate. If you take away his
Catholic background, John F. Kennedy was a traditional American pres-
ident. He was white, male, and from the Northeast. If you take away Joe
Lieberman's Jewish background, he doesn't seem all that different from

Kennedy: white, male, and from the Northeast.

Heck, you can even say our current president—who presents himself as a born-again from Texas—is really not that different from Kennedy or Lieberman: George W. Bush is white, male, and from the Northeast. His family has a home in Kennebunkport, Maine, and he went to Yale, as did the man who ran against him, John Kerry (white, male, from the Northeast).

So 24, having elected two African-American presidents, is pure fantasy, right?

At the moment, yes.

In the future, no.

And I would have written those last two sentences even before Barak Obama burst onto the scene.

TELEVISION AND THE POLITICS OF RACE

A few years ago, the NAACP threatened a boycott of network television. The organization claimed discrimination was rife in the entertainment industry. They claimed that without positive role models of all races, Americans would never even think about the possibility of multi-ethnic leaders at all levels, from business to entertainment to politics. Under threat of that boycott, the networks promised to diversify—although they really haven't.

Why does the NAACP believe the lack of multi-ethnic faces in front of and behind the television cameras matters?

Because the people in charge of the movie studios and the television networks are white. They present a white point of view. Whenever a non-white person gets a role or even a television show, the white bosses want to know why. Why does this character have a black sidekick? Does that mean the character is really liberal?

This attitude extends to news coverage, which is run by the entertainment division. Historically, black candidates got significantly less airtime than white candidates. And less airtime translates into less penetration for the black candidates' message, which translates into a decreased opportunity to attract voters. Black candidates have had to rely on non-traditional outlets and one-on-one appearances to get out their message.

That's changed in the past year. In 2006, a handful of black candidates *did* attract media attention, from Harold Ford Jr. in Tennessee to Barak Obama in Illinois. Superficially, it looks like things are improving.

But the improvements are heartbreakingly slow. Even in today's market, it's okay for a respected white commentator to ask a racist question because the commentator (and his bosses) assumes that the audience wants to hear the answer to that racist question. The audience that he envisions is white, middle class, and uncomfortable with people of color.

Think it doesn't happen routinely? Or on network television with respected commentators? Let's just take the most recent example at the time of this writing.

On May 13, 2007, George Stephanopoulos interviewed Barak Obama. Stephanopoulos asked this question: "You have a very cool style when you're doing those town meetings, when you're on the campaign trail. And I wonder, how much of that is tied to your race?" (*Chicago Sun-Times*).

I wanted Obama to slap Stephanopoulos silly—verbally, of course. Instead, Obama paused, blinked, and said, "That's interesting." And then changed the subject.

Because he values his political career, and he knows he needs so-called liberal whites like Stephanopoulos—who don't even realize that the question is offensive to a large portion of their audience—to get airtime.

Air time. Politics in modern America is all about coverage. And airtime goes to the candidates that the media believe deserve it. Candidates can't be elected without airtime, so they have to struggle to get it.

Obama knew if he had attacked Stephanopoulos for that comment, it would have dominated the news cycle for the next twenty-four hours—and the stories would have been focused on Obama's "oversensitivity," not Stephanopoulos's bigoted question.

Obama has been getting a lot of airtime in 2007. Partly because he's an interesting, charismatic candidate.

And partly, I think, because of the Presidents Palmer.

What we can imagine becomes what we believe in. What we believe in eventually becomes the norm.

So in order to talk about the first real black presidents of the United States—as a ground-breaking television show presents them—we have to discuss why, in 2007, it's so damn unusual—*still*—for any American television show to imagine that a black man can be president of the United States.

To listen to critics talk, you'd think that television is a highly conservative medium. I don't simply mean that in the political sense—although it often is: law and order; good guys vs. bad; *Father Knows Best*—but also in the risk-taking sense. Television, according to the critics, reflects society.

It doesn't change society.

Yeah, right. Uh-huh.

Let's talk television history for a minute.

The first African American to host a network television program was pianist-singer Bob Howard. His show, the creatively titled *The Bob Howard Show*, aired for more than two years, starting in August of 1948 (McNeil 102).

You read that right. 1948. Six years before the official start of what we now call the Civil Rights Movement. The same year that seven-days-a-week, four-network television broadcasting began in New York.[1] The same year that coaxial cables linked the East with the Midwest, making simultaneous national broadcasts a reality—except for those poor folks who lived west of the Mississippi (McNeil 11). Three years before *I Love Lucy*, and six years before the momentous Supreme Court decision *Brown v. Board of Education* desegregated public schools.

A conservative medium? Blacks and whites couldn't attend the same schools, yet African Americans held positions of power on television. And within eighteen months, Bob Howard wasn't the only African American to host a national television show with his name in the title. He was followed by Hazel Scott in 1950 and Billy Daniels in 1952 (McNeil 502).

So if there were three television shows hosted by African Americans and a number of African Americans guest-starring on other television programs by 1952, why did African Americans largely disappear from the airwaves by 1960?

---

[1] Television Central in those dark days was New York City, not Hollywood. Hollywood, way back then, was for movies.

It had nothing to do with the creative minds behind the television series. The writers and producers wanted talented people on their shows, no matter what color. It had nothing to do with a shortage of actors to do the work.

It had everything to do with the great American bugaboos: Money. Power. Greed. And, you guessed it, race.

Even though television was "national" in 1948, it really wasn't. Yes, the shows could be broadcast simultaneously over half the continent, but hardly anyone had a television set. And most of those sets existed in the urban areas of the Northeast—a part of the country where mixed-race couples felt safest (note I did not say safe), a part of the country where multi-ethnic people mixed with whites. Whites were used to hearing many languages and seeing many colors. To most urban north-easterners, the world was multiracial, multilingual, and multicolored.

The rest of America, however, preferred to segregate groups.[2]

By the mid 1950s, television had become a national phenomenon. Consider this: In 1950, there were 43.5 million households in the United States, but only 10 million of them had television sets. By 1960, there were 52.6 million households in the United States, and 45 million of them had televisions (*The New Information Please Almanac* 220, 226).

Those televisions existed in the Deep South as well as in the urban Northeast. They existed in the Upper Midwest and the Intermountain West.

And all over the country, people watched. They filled out little forms testifying to their viewing habits, and companies sponsored television shows as a form of advertising. In fact, a show sponsored by, say, Texaco, only ran Texaco ads during the commercial breaks.

Suddenly, television shows had to appeal to a "nationwide" audience as opposed to a select group. Sid Caesar, who did the classic, important *Your Show of Shows*,[3] has spoken repeatedly about the increasing influence of studio heads and advertisers, who wanted him to drop his "intel-

---

[2] Yes, I know. There was a lot of *de facto* segregation in the urban Northeast. Each group had its neighborhood. But the neighborhoods overlapped, and the faces on the subway were not from one ethnic group. You got used to seeing others who were different from you every single day.

[3] Writers who worked on *Your Show of Shows* included Mel Brooks, Neil Simon, and Woody Allen.

lectual" sketches for things that would appeal to the masses. Caesar fought that battle for nearly a decade before throwing in the towel,[4] but the handwriting was on the wall.

Programming now had to have a national (read: white, middle-class, and high-school educated) focus. And into this mix came *The Nat King Cole Show*.

Television mythology says that Nat King Cole was the first African American to host a nationwide television show. Television mythology also claims he failed. The second claim is as bogus as the first.

Nat King Cole, an extremely successful singer and pianist whose hits "Mona Lisa" and "Route 66" (among others) can still be heard today, got his own variety show in the fall of 1956. The show was canceled after about eighteen episodes because it couldn't attract a sponsor. "Though it was reported that potential sponsors feared a Southern boycott [of their products]," writes Alex McNeil in *Total Television*, "it should be noted that several NBC affiliates in the North as well as the South declined to carry the show" (502).

1956. The year after the Montgomery Bus Boycott made Rosa Parks a household name. The year that the Supreme Court ruled bus segregation unconstitutional. The year before President Eisenhower ordered paratroopers to Little Rock to enforce an order to integrate Central High School.

The country had already spent two years battling what my *Negro Almanac* rightly calls the Civil Rights Revolution (the changes are really too cataclysmic to be called a "movement"), and white folks were already getting tired of it. They didn't want to see any indications of it on their television sets. African Americans, on the other hand, couldn't get jobs in the powerful broadcasting companies or the nationwide advertising companies, which made fighting back nearly impossible.

As a result, the common wisdom after the cancellation of *The Nat King Cole Show* became this: African American performers were sponsor-killers. They "destroyed" revenue. They caused "boycotts." They were bad for business.

So the creative minds behind the shows suddenly heard that certain actors were unacceptable. Too many black faces would destroy a show's chances in the South (and, if you look at McNeil's statement, in the "lib-

---

[4] First on *Your Show of Shows* and then on *Caesar's Hour*.

eral" North as well).

The problem with that is that over time common wisdom becomes accepted as fact—not just in television, or movies, or politics, but in literature as well. As late as 1997, the accepted wisdom in another branch of the entertainment industry, publishing, was this: African Americans did not buy books. If African Americans did buy books, they only bought books written by African American authors. White readers would never buy a book about an African American.

How do I know this was common wisdom as late as 1997? Because, naïve me, I wrote a mystery novel set in 1968 with a male African-American detective as my first person point-of-view character. This was back in the days when Oprah Winfrey's book club sold enough copies of each chosen book to fund a publishing company's year, and publishing executives seemed to believe that she would favor a book by African Americans over one by whites (even though early statistics did not bear this out; she liked *good books* no matter who wrote them).

When I finished *Dangerous Road*, which I wrote under the pen name Kris Nelscott, publishing companies tripped all over themselves to offer me six-figure deals. One was pending when my agent was asked if I could tour (meaning: Was I personable enough to go on *Oprah*?). My agent called me, telling me that the publishing company thought the author was an African-American man who had been a pioneer in the Civil Rights Movement (in other words, they thought I was a sixty-five-year-old African-American man). What should she do? Tell them the truth, I said.

The truth is that I'm a middle-aged white woman who watched those televised early civil rights protests from my playpen.

The minute the publishing companies discovered this fact, they withdrew their offers. A white woman, they believed, couldn't write a book that would appeal to African Americans.

Never mind that the books in the series, which St. Martin's eventually took a risk with, have been nominated for the prestigious Edgar Award as well as this year's Shamus Award, and have been chosen six separate times as the best mystery novel of the year. Never mind that people of all colors have bought the series and loved it.

Common wisdom. It's a lovely cover for all kinds of bigotry. Pioneers all over the entertainment industry have fought against this common wisdom, but it isn't just an uphill battle. It's a hike across the Alps.

Black faces became more common in the 1970s and the 1980s. By the 1990s, almost every television show had an African-American co-star. But African Americans rarely held positions of power in entertainment programming, and when they did, they were clearly tokens. There were a few African-American presidents and a few African-American executives on television programs, but they had minor, often non-speaking roles. Their faces had become a politically correct way of pretending that the studios were trying to represent America on the screen.

So it wasn't until 2001, when David Palmer debuted on *24*, that we actually had, in the words of Dennis Haysbert, "the first African American president on television in a three-dimensional role" ("24").

"How ironic that the network that's pegged as the one for and by neo-conservatives, Fox, has the foresight to cast African Americans as president of their award-winning drama, *24*," says Stephen Braunginn. Braunginn, who has worked for a whole host of liberal organizations and was influential in the Reverend Jesse Jackson's 1988 political campaign, is a fan of *24* despite its conservative reputation. While the show gets a little too "torturific" for him at times, he loves the positive light in which it portrays African Americans (Braunginn).

That light is still too rare, fifty years after NBC pulled the plug on *The Nat King Cole Show*. Even though the United States is a vastly different nation than the one that existed in 1956, those differences are only now starting to show up in the entertainment industry.

"I have witnessed a profound shift in race relations in my lifetime," writes Barak Obama, who was born in 1961. "I have felt it as surely as one feels a change in the temperature.

"But," he cautions, "as much as I insist that things have gotten better, I am mindful of this truth as well: Better isn't good enough" (Obama 233).

Not in life, and not in life's reflector, television.

So how do things get better?

One dream at a time.

THE TRIUMPH OF IMAGINATION

Robert Cochran and Joel Surnow, who wrote the pilot script for *24*, have wisely never said why they decided to make David Palmer African American. (Isn't it interesting that we even have to ask the question of why? It still shows how unusual an African-American president is, especially since he's the creation of white writers.) If I had to guess, I would surmise they did it purely for plot reasons.

Throughout his campaign, David Palmer is threatened with assassination. Television writers have to use shorthand to make their point. How can they convince you that one presidential candidate is more vulnerable to assassination than another? Unfortunately, in today's world, all they have to do is make him African American.

When Jesse Jackson ran for president, he received so many death threats that the Secret Service made him wear a bulletproof vest everywhere he went ("What We Learned"). Obama automatically received Secret Service protection, a service not offered to most presidential candidates until they've secured the nomination of their party ("Is America Ready?").[5]

Former Secretary of State Colin Powell was drafted by the Republican Party in 1996 to run against President Bill Clinton. Powell, who was probably the only possible Republican candidate who could have matched Clinton charisma for charisma, intelligence for intelligence, and experience for experience,[6] turned the offer down because his wife asked him not to run. She was afraid he would be assassinated (Harnden).

Politically aware Americans know all of that. So as the Palmer assassination attempts evolved, viewers assumed the attempts were motivated by Palmer's race (indeed, CTU agents discussed this repeatedly). The fact that the threat came from something other than a bigoted wacko was yet another refreshing change in American television.

But whatever the reasons for making David Palmer an African American, the result was electrifying. Palmer became, in the words of co-star D. B. Woodside, "the heart of the show" ("24").

David Palmer became the heart of the show for two reasons: the way his character is written, and Dennis Haysbert himself.

David Palmer, as written, is not a token or a symbol. He has good qualities and bad. He's not perfect. He is, in the words of Associated

---

[5] Some critics find the *Newsweek* article itself to be a problem. "*Newsweek*'s batting this question around creates doubt in Americans' minds," says Braunginn in an e-mail interview. "They're guilty of pulling out the race . . . card."

[6] *Newsweek* actually says that Colin Powell "might well have won had he run in 1996" (32).

Press reporter Frazier Moore, "strong and heroic " (Moore). But he's also "a perfectly believable politician," which the *New York Times* defines as "both statesmanlike and crafty" (James).

This is an incredible balancing act. African Americans would not watch the show if David Palmer had been an evil man. In fact, such a portrayal would have been cliché in the 1960s—a black man was still considered inferior in those days, and either he would have been portrayed as not up for the task or as venal and corrupt.

In modern times, no self-respecting black actor would have played an evil David Palmer. It is still a dream to have a black man in such a position of power, and the first black man to become president had to be ethical and good.

David Palmer exists because of a synergy between the character the writers imagined and the character Dennis Haysbert embodied. The casting directors knew that Haysbert was the right man for the job when they saw the dignity he carried in his six-foot four-inch frame and when they heard "that voice" ("24").

Haysbert, for his part, knew the moment he was cast that he had an important job to do.

In a 2002 television interview, he said, "First African American president on prime time television—ever. There's a responsibility that comes with that" ("24").

That line about responsibility sounds like the interview garbage that actors spew, but Haysbert meant it. And he meant it because of who he is and when he was born.

Dennis Haysbert was born in 1954, the year scholars mark as the start of the Civil Rights movement. He was born into a world of segregated public buildings. A world of segregated schools. A world in which the second line in the child's rhyme "Eeny-Meany-Miney-Mo" was not "catch a tiger by the toe" but "catch a nigger by the toe." A world in which beatings and lynchings happened with unbelievable frequency. A world in which those beatings and lynchings were often facilitated or in fact conducted by the police.

"Growing up in the '50s and '60s in LA," says novelist and commentator Steven Barnes, "every president looked like the men who once owned my family as well as almost everyone I saw on television or in film, the faces on every piece of money in my pocket, the governor of every state" (Barnes).

It was a dispiriting, hopeless world for a black child, a world best described by Dr. Martin Luther King Jr. in his famous "Letter from Birmingham Jail":

> . . . you suddenly find your tongue twisted and your speech stammering as you seek to explain to your six-year-old daughter why she can't go to the public amusement park that has just been advertised on television, and see tears welling up in her little eyes when she is told that Funtown is closed to colored children, and see the depressing clouds of inferiority begin to form in her little mental sky, and see her begin to distort her little personality by unconsciously developing a bitterness toward white people; when you have to concoct an answer for a five-year-old son asking in agonizing pathos: "Daddy, why do white people treat colored people so mean?" . . . (Martin Luther King Jr. 267)

African-American commentators from Stanley Crouch to Steven Barnes have commented on the debilitating effect this upbringing had on the children of the time. Dr. King touches on it when he mentions the "depressing clouds of inferiority" that cause his daughter to distort her personality to reflect the reality of racism (Alter 33, Barnes).

Barak Obama also mentions the effects of racism on blacks in *The Audacity of Hope*, and points out that while things have changed, they haven't changed enough.

> While my own upbringing hardly typifies the African American experience[7]—and, although largely through luck and circumstance, I now occupy a position that insulates me from most of the bumps and bruises that the average black man must endure—I can recite the usual litany of petty slights that during my forty-five years have been directed my way: security guards tailing me as I shop in department

---

[7] Obama was raised by a white mother in multiracial communities in Hawaii and Indonesia.

stores, white couples who toss me their car keys as I stand outside a restaurant waiting for the valet, police cars pulling me over for no apparent reason. I know what it's like to have people tell me I can't do something because of my color. . . . (Obama 233)

Haysbert, who is seven years older than Obama and who, unlike Obama, was raised in the United States, has experienced all of these things and more. In California, where Haysbert was born, neighborhood covenants in wealthy and middle-class areas prevented home owners from selling to African Americans.[8] Haysbert was twelve years old when violence tore apart the black neighborhood of Watts in Los Angeles, and fourteen when Dr. King was assassinated.

It was with this background and in this environment that Haysbert entered the world of professional acting. His role models were few: Bill Cosby, Sidney Poitier, Ozzie Davis, and Paul Robeson were the only nationally recognizable African-American dramatic actors in 1970 (*The Negro Almanac* 815–848).[9]

With such a dearth of role models, a recent question AP reporter Frazier Moore asked Haysbert seems a lot more relevant: What made the young Haysbert believe that he could make a go of acting?

Haysbert's answer was simple and stark. "Tenacity. I kept believing I could do it. That being black didn't matter, and that if I had the talent, I should be able to do what I wanted to do" (Moore 3).

His attitude was extremely unusual at the time, but it was a growing one. The 1970s saw a sea change in that television attitude toward black performers. Oprah Winfrey got her start during that decade. Samuel L. Jackson, Morgan Freeman, and Denzel Washington all became actors in those years, though they wouldn't achieve success for more than a decade. They were following on the heels of Sidney Poitier and the handful of other

---

[8] Even though these clauses were nullified by successful lawsuits in the late 1960s and early 1970s, they still existed into the 1980s. There was a minor scandal when reporters discovered that then-President Ronald Reagan's favorite ranch still had such a covenant in place.

[9] Note that Louis Gosset Jr., James Earl Jones, and Harry Belafonte are mentioned in this thirty-year-old volume, but are (in 1976) just at the beginning of their decades-long careers. James Earl Jones's breakout role in *The Great White Hope* didn't hit film until after 1970.

role models, but it took a lot of perseverance—and a deeply ingrained knowledge of how hard it was to fight against the casual racism that was evolving from the violent racism of the pre–Civil Rights era.

So when Haysbert talks about the responsibility he holds in portraying the first African-American president of the United States, he speaks from hard-won experience.

And he knew, like any other black actor of his generation would have known, the tightrope he walked in portraying the first black president of the United States.

Most black presidents as portrayed in the media are based on the Martin Luther King model—a man who is religious, who is a brilliant and charismatic speaker, and who wears his ethics on his sleeve. A man who is willing to die for his cause.

David Palmer was not religious (that we knew of), although he was brilliant and charismatic. He struggled with his ethics, but he always made the right choice for the country.

David Palmer had a firm moral compass. He knew what to do when politics and morals clashed, which was what made him the heart of the show. When faced with a tough choice, he avoided the politically expedient solution and pursued the moral one.

Few modern politicians have done that, and almost all have paid a high price for their moral choices. Lyndon Baines Johnson, for all his horrible choices in Vietnam, forced Congress to pass a tougher version of the Civil Rights legislation that John F. Kennedy only tepidly supported. As a result of passing history-making legislation that has helped change this country for the better, Johnson lost the white South for the Democrats for the next forty years, and helped to ensure Republican victories for such lovely candidates as the racist Jesse Helms.

George McGovern came out strongly against the Vietnam war in 1972. His stance proved to be the correct one, but he lost every race except Massachusetts and Washington, D.C., in his doomed election campaign.

David Palmer paid a high price for his ethics as well. In season three, he refused to fire his brother Wayne for Wayne's affair with the wife of one of the president's major financial backers. For once, Wayne Palmer knew the correct response: firing him would help Palmer politically.

But Palmer valued loyalty above all else, and he loved his brother. Palmer figured he could keep the political damage at a minimum, but he quickly lost control of the situation—partly because he didn't understand its severity. Then he asked his ex-wife to solve the problem quietly. That night, she took advantage of a situation to commit murder—thus making the initial problem go away, but creating a much larger one.

Palmer finally had to refuse to run for a second term—knowing that he could easily be brought up on charges of conspiracy to commit murder because of his ex-wife's actions, actions he did not—and would not have—approved.

It was an uncomfortable moment for everyone from the characters to the 24 staff to the viewers. Because Palmer couldn't be corrupt. It wouldn't follow the character. He had to make the good and moral choice, even if it was the wrong choice for him.

His mistakes—his human mistakes, in trusting someone he once loved—were understandable; his solution was heartbreaking, particularly considering his status as the first black president.

But season three had some other interesting moments that concern race. Season three portrayed how anyone who works in politics must compromise. Palmer's leading financial supporter, Alan Milliken, was a true money man, one who thought he'd "bought" his favorite politician.

Such comments would have been offensive coming from the mouth of a white financier. The very thought of a white man "buying" a black man in 2007 still has too many echoes to our country's disgraceful beginnings, built on slavery.

I'm sure that's why Milliken was black—to avoid a politically incorrect moment. But the result allowed the show to speak some truth. Since the mid-nineteenth century, there have been black millionaires.[10] That century also saw the rise of black colleges.[11] Those colleges were started to give blacks a fighting chance in the world of intellect, a chance they rarely got at white colleges.[12]

---

[10] No one knows who the first African-American millionaire was, but most reference books put Thomy Gafon, a real-estate speculator and moneylender in Louisiana, as the first. He had his fortune in place by 1890.

[11] Most were founded after the Civil War. However, the first black college founded in the United States was Cheyney State in Pennsylvania, founded in 1837.

[12] For an interesting look at the influence these black colleges have, watch *Stomp the Yard*, last summer's surprise hit. The movie is filled with black actors, dealing with the black experience, and looking at the importance of education. Pay particular attention during the scenes in Heritage Hall.

A black middle class also arose and protected its children from the harshness of racism. They created a community of black professionals, crossing into the white world only when necessary. You could go from birth (at a black-run hospital) to death (at a black-run funeral home) and rarely interact with whites.

Political campaigns like Jesse Jackson's, like Barak Obama's, get funded by wealthy blacks as well as wealthy whites. And those wealthy blacks have an agenda, just like Alan Milliken did. 24's producers knew that David Palmer wouldn't get to be president without making some difficult moral compromises—and that meant the occasional strange bedfellow.

By season three, also, we learned that David Palmer existed less on the Martin Luther King model than he did on the Kennedy model. John F. Kennedy's campaign manager was his brother Robert, who, in 1960, was an extremely controversial figure. Robert was a devout practicing Catholic, more or less faithful to his wife Ethel (rare not just in politics, but in the Kennedy family).

But in politics he was, as some called him, a ruthless son of a bitch. When JFK became president, he took nepotism to a new level and made his brother attorney general. Together they stood against the Washington establishment, and worked with one another on tough issues, like Civil Rights.

JFK.used his brother Robert as a hatchet man. When someone had to deliver harsh news, it was always Robert. Robert took it on himself to go after the mob in those years—and the mob had had considerable influence in getting JFK elected, particularly in Chicago.[13]

Americans have forgotten this over time. They have forgotten it because JFK's assassination changed Robert. He spiraled into a deep depression, then went on a pilgrimage and discovered a new cause—poverty.

When Robert ran for president, he was assassinated, just like his brother. And also like his brother, he is remembered as a saint.

Wayne Palmer is not Robert Kennedy. He's not a happily married

---

[13] And let's not mention one of the many women JFK slept with during the campaign, a woman who was the girlfriend of Sam Giancana, a major Chicago mobster. Giancana wanted to use that against Kennedy, although he wasn't able to do so during the truncated years of the Kennedy administration.

Catholic who had a moral awakening. As portrayed by D.B. Woodside, he's not as smart or as ethical as his brother, when in fact Robert was probably smarter and (by the end) more ethical than JFK.

But the hand-in-glove metaphor worked. David Palmer would not have become president without his somewhat shady brother. And David Palmer's assassination was Wayne's moral awakening.

Robert Kennedy never got a chance to put that moral awakening into practice. Wayne Palmer learned that wanting to do good and actually doing good are two very different things.

All of the seeds for season six's lessons were planted in season three. And season three is when the writers truly stopped being afraid of their black president and started using him to the fullest—as a human being.

We need to see people of color as human beings. Because that's when we stop seeing them as "black" people—and start seeing them as people.

Television—and characters like the Palmer brothers—are one way of achieving that goal.

IT'S NOT JUST THE MEDIUM; IT'S THE MESSAGE

Obama mentions the power of television in passing. He writes: "I know as well that Michelle and I must be continually vigilant against some of the debilitating story lines that our daughters may absorb—from TV and music and friends and the streets—about who the world thinks they are, and what the world imagines they should be" (Obama 233).

The last point is the most important: *what the world imagines they should be*. Ideas affect everyone, and so do images.

While I researched this essay, Senator Joseph Biden announced that he was going to run for president, and in practically the same breath, he praised Senator Obama as a good competitor for the office because he is the first African-American candidate for president who is "articulate" and "clean."

I never heard anyone complain that Shirley Chisholm, Carol Mosley Braun, the Reverend Jesse Jackson, and the Reverend Al Sharpton weren't clean. Nor could you call any of them inarticulate. Biden does not consider himself racist, but his ideas come from some deeply held assumptions. He meant what he said, and the ironic thing is that he meant it as a *compliment*, not understanding until the press jumped on him how he had insulted not just the previous presidential candidates, but an entire race of people.

In the past, the media always blocked the message that African Americans could be viable political candidates of any sort. You only have to go back twenty years to understand how difficult it was for an African-American candidate to get his message across.[14]

"I won a lot of press attention, but not always because my ideas were being taken seriously," says the Reverend Jesse L. Jackson, who ran for president in 1984 and 1988. "Some couldn't see past the novelty of an African-American running for president" (Ferraro and Jackson 40).

But it's not as great a novelty anymore, thanks in part to Jackson, Braun, and others. We must attribute some of that sea of change, however, to 24.[15] For three seasons (and part of a fourth), Americans watched as a capable person ran the United States.

A capable person who was male and from the Northeast. A person who also happened to be African American.

The *New York Times* put this in perspective in its review of the second-season opener: "David Palmer is the first black president of the United States, but no one seems to notice. The matter-of-fact way 24 has placed him in the White House just hints at how this clever suspense series . . . toys with and enhances reality" (James).

Unlike the mainstream media, 24 didn't make Palmer's blackness a plotline. They used it to add tension but it was subtle, and they twisted it. Palmer wasn't threatened because of his skin color. He was threatened because Victor Drazen wanted revenge on both Palmer and Jack Bauer for something that happened in Kosovo two years before, an incident that had nothing to do with race.

That casual acceptance of something America currently doesn't casu-

---

[14] Or maybe only three years. Why did no reporter give Carol Mosley Braun, the first African-American woman elected to the U.S. Senate, the courtesy of covering her presidential campaign with anything other than contempt? Because she was African American? Because she was a woman? Because she was an African-American woman? Her message is no different from Barak Obama's, and she has great charisma in person. So why was she covered so differently?

[15] I'm not the only one who thinks this. Moore of AP writes, "He was strong and heroic as President David Palmer, the nation's first black chief executive, in a performance that surely got Americans thinking such a thing in real life isn't so farfetched, and is maybe overdue" (Moore 3).

ally accept creates an idealized country. And that idealism is important.

So important, in fact, that it's one of the reasons people signed on to work on 24.

"One of the things that I thought was the most powerful thing [in reading the first script] was that we have an African American president," said Kiefer Sutherland in a recent interview. "I believe theater and film and television [are] really that powerful, and if you show . . . African American people in this kind of position of political power, then people will believe that it is possible. I thought that was a very positive statement" ("Kiefer Sutherland").

THE DEATH OF DAVID PALMER

If it's so important to have a character like David Palmer in a position of power, then why in the world would the writers assassinate him at the start of season five?

"I think it was a mistake," Haysbert said in a 2006 interview. "It buys into the legacy of the country. Every charismatic, wonderful leader we've ever had—they've shot him. And we could've broken that legacy by letting David Palmer live on" ("Once Commander in Chief").

Initially, I agreed. I never read about a show before I watch it, so I was extremely unprepared for the first ten minutes of season five. I paused my TiVo at the commercial break and worried about the political implications.

They had assassinated President Palmer—and he wasn't even president any longer.

But I continued (how could anyone fail to continue after that slam-bang opening?), and found that I agreed with D. B. Woodside.

"Honestly," he said, "I thought at first they were making a big mistake" ("24").

Note that he said *at first*. Then the season progressed. Charles Logan, played by Gregory Itzin, looked like Nixon and acted like the popular perception of George W. Bush: weak, wishy-washy, and a victim of his advisors. In the end, Logan became a true villain—and the last episode of the season, as he was arrested while President Palmer's casket headed toward its final rest, was one of the most powerful statements about morality and politics I have ever seen on television.

Who would you rather have as president: someone like Charles Logan or someone like David Palmer? The entire country—neoconservatives to the radical left—would agree: David Palmer is our ideal president.

And *24* elevated him even more—not because he was African American, but because he was a good man.

Haysbert also says in that interview that allowing Palmer to live would have given "the show somewhere to go" ("Once Commander in Chief").

And if the writers weren't so good, I would have agreed with him. But Palmer's death allowed *24* to step into territory never seen in the movies, on television, or, heck, even in literature.

24 had just inaugurated . . .

THE SECOND AFRICAN-AMERICAN PRESIDENT OF THE UNITED STATES

With just as little fanfare as with the first African-American president, *24* has made television history.

But it's a history that went unnoticed as fans clutched the edges of their seats throughout season six. Wayne Palmer is a known quantity. He's not as ethical as his brother. He's more realistic. And he's a little more human. He screws up in new and creative ways.

After the horrible experience of Charles Logan's presidency and the death of David Palmer, the country has clearly turned to Wayne for healing, thinking that the brother of one man is the same as the man himself.

"I think [Wayne is] constantly following in his brother's footsteps and his brother was a man who was extremely noble, full of a lot of integrity," said D. B. Woodside in a recent interview. "I think Wayne is the same way but . . . he d[oes]n't exactly have the temperament for the job. He ha[s] the intelligence, he ha[s] the know-how, but his temperament is something he's going to have to continue to work on as this day goes on" ("Kiefer Sutherland").

Wayne's very human dilemma makes for interesting television. His presence as the second African-American president makes him as unusual as our second president, John Adams. Adams isn't remembered as a great man like George Washington. George Washington was the first. He defined the role. Adams was simply the second in a long line of presidents trying to live up to Washington's example.

As, I hope, Wayne Palmer will. The more people of color we see on the screen in positions of power, the more we will come to accept nonwhites in all situations. The medium is the message, sure, but it's also the future.

What we can imagine we can become.

We can imagine a country where it is commonplace to elect African Americans president.

We can become that country—maybe as early as 2008.

And when we do, we can finally fulfill the vision articulated by one of this country's greatest leaders, Dr. King. We can finally start, as *24* already does, judging people "not by the color of their skin but by the content of their character" (Martin Luther King Jr. 82).

KRISTINE KATHRYN RUSCH writes mystery novels about 1960s black detective Smokey Dalton under the name Kris Nelscott. Those novels have been nominated for the Edgar, the Shamus, and several other awards. As Kristine Kathryn Rusch, she writes science fiction and fantasy. While most readers ask Nelscott how she can write from the perspective of a black man, no one asks Rusch how she can write from the point of view of an elf.

REFERENCES

"24." *E! True Hollywood Story.* Season 11, Episode 24. E!, 13 Jan. 2007.

Alter, Johnathan. "Is America Ready?": *Newsweek*, December 25, 2006–January 1, 2007, 32–33.

Barnes, Steven. "Obama's Future, Free of an American Past?" *All Things Considered*, NPR, 11 Dec. 2006.

Braunginn, Stephen. E-mail to the author. 20 Jan. 2007.

"The Black Entertainer in the Performing Arts." *The Negro Almanac: A Reference Work on the Afro American.* Third Edition. Bellwether Publishing, 1976. 815–848.

Ferraro, Geraldine, and Reverend Jesse L. Jackson. "What We Learned the Hard Way": *Newsweek*, December 25, 2006–January 1, 2007, 40.

Harnden, Toby. "Wife's Ultimatum to Powell: If You Run I'll Leave." *The Telegraph*, 11 Nov. 2002. <www.telegraph.co.uk/news/main.jhtml=/

news/2002/11/21/wusa21.xml>

James, Caryn. "Television Review: Clock Reset, Agent Bauer Returns to Work." *The New York Times*, 29 Oct. 2002.

"Kiefer Sutherland." *Larry King Live.* CNN, 9 Jan. 2007.

King, Martin Luther, Jr. "I Have a Dream." In *The Norton Anthology of African American Literature*, edited by Henry Louis Gates, Jr., and Nellie Y. McKay, 82. New York: W.W. Norton and Company, 1997.

King, Martin Luther, Jr. "Letter from a Birmingham Jail." In *The Best American Essays of the Century*, edited by Joyce Carol Oates and Robert Atwan, 267. New York: Houghton Mifflin, 2000.

McNeil, Alex. *Total Television: A Comprehensive Guide to Programming from 1948 to 1980.* New York: Penguin, 1980.

Moore, Frazier. "Haysbert Creates Indelible Image as a Man of Action." *The Oregonian*, 17 Dec. 2006.

The Negro Almanac: A Reference Work on the Afro American. Third Edition. Bellwether Publishing, 1976.

The New Information Please Almanac Atlas and Yearbook 1965. Nineteenth edition. New York: Simon and Schuster, 1964.

Obama, Barak. *The Audacity of Hope.* New York: Crown Publishers, 2006.

"Once Commander in Chief, Dennis Haysbert Now a Commando in 'The Unit.'" *The TV Tattler.* 10 Apr. 2006. <www.television.aol.com/tv_tattler_celebrity_interviews/dennis-haysbert>

Sweet, Lynn. "Obama on ABC's 'This Week with George Stephanopoulos.'" *Chicago Sun-Times*, 13 May 2007. <blogs.suntimes.com/sweet/2007/05/obama_on_abcs_this_week_with_g.html>

Jack Bauer Syndrome

ERIC GREENE

If you're looking to us for realistic advice on how to fight terrorism we're all in real trouble.

—*24* Co-Creator Robert Cochran

You say that nuclear devices have gone off in the United
States, more are planned, and we're wondering about whether
waterboarding would be a bad thing to do? I'm looking for
Jack Bauer at that time!

—Congressman Tom Tancredo,
Republican Presidential Candidate Debate, May 15, 2007

Sometimes . . . you have to do . . . terrible things, even unforgivable things, for the sake of your country.

—Graem Bauer, *24* (6-7)

During the May 15, 2007, Republican Presidential primary
debate, conservative newscaster Brit Hume posed the following
version of the oft-cited "ticking time bomb" hypothetical: three

171

suicide bombings have killed hundreds of Americans and "a fourth attack has been averted when the attackers were captured . . . and taken to Guantanamo. . . . U.S. intelligence believes that another, larger attack is planned. . . . How aggressively would you interrogate [the captured suspects]?"

In response, Congressman Tom Tancredo assured the crowd—to enthusiastic applause—that he would be "looking for Jack Bauer at that time." Tancredo invoked no historical precedent, military commander, or interrogation expert. Rather, this United States Congressman and candidate for Commander-in-Chief instead declared his reliance on a TV character. Tancredo was reduced to relying on a fictional hero because real-world historians, military commanders, and interrogators largely oppose torture as illegal, immoral, and ineffective.[1]

And while ever-present in America's torture debate, the ticking bomb scenario is as fictional as Jack Bauer.[2] Among other problems, ticking bomb hypotheticals assume, at minimum, 1) a capture 2) before an attack 3) of a prisoner who actually possesses, rather than is just suspected of possessing, 4) actionable information 5) that s/he can be coerced into revealing 6) in time for it to help prevent or minimize damage. None of these assumptions are very sound.

A year before Tancredo's play for the Jack Bauer vote, on June 23, 2006, an unusual event unfolded at the Heritage Foundation, one of America's most prominent conservative think tanks: elites from the world of politics, punditry, and pop culture gathered for a symposium entitled "24 and America's Image in Fighting Terrorism: Fact, Fiction, or Does It Matter?" Moderated by Rush Limbaugh, the panel brought 24 creators, producers, writers, and cast members together with national security experts, and was preceded by an address by Secretary of Homeland Security Michael Chertoff, perhaps the first time a White House cabinet member has publicly addressed the political relevance of a TV series. Front and center in the audience was

---

[1] In fact, the Bush administration policies on torture were said to have been resisted by experts in the FBI and the military. See, for example, Stuart Taylor's "How Not to Make Terrorism Policy," and Scott Shane and Mark Mazzetti's "Advisers Fault Harsh Methods in Interrogation."

[2] Literally. Political science professor Darius Rejali has noted that the first appearance of the ticking time bomb concept was in 1960, in Jean Larteguy's Les Centurions, a novel about the French occupation of Algeria (Mayer).

Supreme Court Judge Clarence Thomas, whose wife, a 24 fan, had conceived the symposium.

Jim Carafano, a Heritage Foundation national security scholar, opened the discussion by declaring that the ticking time bomb scenario "has nothing to do with reality. I was in the army for twenty-five years. I've talked to lots of people who have been in lots of wars; I've talked to lots of law enforcement. I've never yet found anyone that's ever confronted the ticking time bomb scenario. . . . [T]hat scenario, as far as I can tell, has never even happened in human history." He went on to say that what 24 models is "not how you stop terrorists. Actually it's the worst thing you'd want." Here, at the start of what was largely a celebration of 24, was an emphatic repudiation of the very premise on which 24, a conservative favorite, is based. And this came from someone who works for the *Heritage Foundation*.

But while it makes for a flawed thought experiment, the ticking bomb scenario, with its high stakes, compressed time, and critical decisions of life, death, and morality, can make for compelling drama. Surnow, however, clings to the ticking bomb formula as more than a story telling device but as moral instruction: with a faith unsullied by facts ("we've had all these torture experts come by recently, and they say . . . torture doesn't work. But I don't believe that," he told writer Jane Mayer), he insisted to the conservative *Washington Times* that "if there's a bomb about to hit a major U.S. city and you have a person with information . . . if you don't torture that person, that would be one of the most immoral acts you could imagine" (Tapper).

Taking that assertion at face value still leaves us with questions: How imminent must the threat be before torture is warranted, even required? Can we torture to stop a bomb that is not yet ticking but we believe will tick eventually, say, a bomb that may be planted in a year? Two years?

How much certainty do we need before we torture? Absolute certainty? Or will strong suspicion suffice? Can we torture if we don't have evidence but still *know* the prisoner is guilty? The same way we "knew" that the federal building in Oklahoma City was bombed by Muslims in 1995? Or the way that we "knew" that Richard Jewel was behind the bombings at the Atlanta Olympics in 1996? Or the way that we "knew" that dozens of the prisoners held in Guantanamo Bay for years without trial were, in Donald Rumsfeld's words, "the worst of the worst" before

173

they were cleared and released?[3] Or the way that jurors and judges "knew" that the over 200 wrongfully convicted people who have been released from America's prisons—and death rows—in recent years, many after being proved factually innocent, were guilty?

Let's say we've answered these questions to everyone's satisfaction and we have adopted an error-proof "torture-is-a-o.k.-in-the-case-of-a-ticking-time-bomb" policy. We've even added a degree of accountability by establishing a system of narrowly tailored torture warrants. What about dangers that are not quite ticking bombs but are significantly *like* ticking bombs? If, as Surnow argues, it would be immoral *not* to torture in the case of a ticking bomb, would it not be equally immoral not to torture in the face of other serious threats?

Given the damage done to our communities by the drug trade, should we torture low-level drug dealers to get them to give up their suppliers? Should we torture uncooperative corporate managers in cases where hundreds or thousands have been harmed or may be harmed by a toxin in the water supply, a pathogen in the food supply, or a medication known by the manufacturer to cause heart attacks?[4]

Should we torture as punishment and deterrent? How about torturing the perpetrators of white collar crimes that undermine our political or financial institutions? Should vice presidential aide Scooter Libby have been tortured to find out if Dick Cheney was behind exposing Valerie Plame's identity as a CIA employee? If we had publicly tortured the perpetrators of the S&L scandal in the '80s, might we have discouraged the directors of Enron from willfully bringing financial ruin to their victims a dozen years later?

Where is the limiting principle in the ticking bomb scenario? Where are the breaks on the slippery slope? Where is the morally coherent rationale to torture in order to prevent some types of grave harm but not others? And if there is a rationale for limiting torture to a finite set of extraordinary circumstances, how do we prevent the exception from

---

[3] For some sobering insight into the national shame that is Guantanamo, see Dahlia Lithwick's "Invisible Men."

[4] Lest you dismiss this as outlandish, consider China's recent execution of the former head of its Food and Drug Administration for taking bribes, an execution the *New York Times* described as part of China's attempt to show that it is serious about improving the safety of Chinese products (Kahn).

swallowing the rule? You need only look at the history of the expansion of the death penalty to realize that the idea of special circumstances is elastic and easily stretched once a precedent has been established. In time the extraordinary tends to become the ordinary. Once we accept torture as policy, how do we prevent a cascade of brutality from coursing through our society?

Complicating the discussion—or making it moot—is the evidence suggesting that torture may not work. Tony Lagouranis, an Army interrogator stationed at Abu Ghraib in 2004 who has admitted to using dogs, sleep deprivation, hypothermia, and dietary manipulations—methods he recalled were *mild* compared to what else was happening—noted that these methods were all ineffective. Lagouranis told the *New Yorker's* Jane Mayer that "in Iraq I never saw pain produce intelligence." In fact, he and other experts argued that "physical pain can strengthen the resolve to clam up." Alternatively, experts argue that torture victims are apt to say whatever they think their tormentors want to hear in order to make the pain stop.[5] Senator John McCain recalls that when physically coerced by his captors to provide the names of his flight squadron he "gave them the names of the Green Bay Packers' offensive line, knowing that providing them false information was sufficient to suspend the abuse" (McCain).[6] So it would seem that if there were a ticking bomb poised to go off, a "President Tancredo" would probably be wasting his time looking for Jack Bauer.

This all leaves us with a perplexing phenomenon: the ticking bomb scenario bears scant resemblance to reality, is denounced by experts, and does little to advance our understanding of the ethical, legal, and policy implications of torture. Yet it persists. And it persists not only in our

---

[5] This is one of the causes of false confessions, which lead to wrongful convictions, in our criminal justice system. Under the pressure of custody and interrogation, even in conditions that fall far short of torture, prisoners have falsely confessed simply to get relief from the psychological and emotional stress.

[6] McCain's story suggests one of the ways torture can backfire—as it apparently has spectacularly in the case of Ibn al-Shaykh al-Libi, a captured Libyan al-Qaeda operative who had been cooperating with CIA interrogators but who, apparently under torture by Egyptian authorities at our behest, "revealed" that Saddam Hussein's Iraq had trained al-Qaeda in the use of weapons of mass destruction. He later recanted, but not before this charge became a key tenet in the Bush Administration's "case" for invading Iraq. And, well, you know the rest.

popular culture, but also in our presidential campaigns. Why? Myths, stereotypes, and misconceptions survive not to the extent that they are true but to the extent that they are, to someone, *useful*.

The secret to the durability of this particular myth, in part, lies in the fact that the ticking bomb scenario is not *about* understanding the torture debate. Rather it is about shutting that debate down. Indeed, the ticking bomb scenario is constructed to be undebatable. The ticking bomb hypothetical is about obscuring genuine policy and ethical controversies by eliminating as inconceivable or insane any options *other* than torture. It is about standing our sense of right and wrong on its head by using the emotional forced perspective of storytelling to create an inexorable narrative "logic" that leads to an execrable conclusion. The ticking bomb scenario is, as suggested by Surnow, about rendering torture the *only* moral choice.

Surnow boldly announced that position at the beginning of 24's second season. The first episode of that season began with South Korean interrogators torturing a captive. The torturers' identifiably Asian features were prominently displayed as they loomed over their victim, his face and race initially obscured, his arms outstretched as in a crucifixion. Immediately a question emerged: Why South Korea? Koreans after all had nothing to do with the rest of the plot. Why was this scene not in Los Angeles or Guantanamo or Riyadh or Washington, D.C.?

The racial, and implied religious, dynamics of the scene were as important as they were deliberate: American fears of torture, specifically at the hands of Asians and especially Communist Asians, span generations through lurid Yellow Peril fantasies, World War II propaganda, and Cold War anxieties. A steady diet of pop culture images of sadistic Asians torturing Westerners—be it the North Koreans in the recent James Bond adventure *Die Another Day*, Vietnamese in *Rambo* and *The Deer Hunter*, "Red" Chinese in *The Manchurian Candidate*, Japanese in *The Bridge on the River Kwai*, or countless other examples over several decades—would likely have provided audiences with ready-made moral and political coordinates for comprehending the torture scene and the "savage" nature of our enemies: "We" know what "they" do. To "us."

But once the Asian torturer stereotype was invoked, the initial understanding of the scene shifted: the prisoner broke, revealed the desired information, and a shaken North Korean interrogator rushed to make his report, at which point the audience was surprised, or was supposed to be surprised, to learn that his masters were not villainous Asians, but White Americans. Perfectly calm. Quietly intent.

This dark and elaborate scene was not about setting up the season's story—in fact, the sequence was narratively irrelevant to the rest of the plot. Rather, this opening was about staking out a position for *24* in a growing national debate about how we should fight the War on Terrorism. The message was clear: "Yes, *we're* the torturers now. This is what it takes. This is what will work. What was once the domain of the savage is now *our* domain. Get used to it."

That message has been consistently reinforced by Jack Bauer's increasingly extreme actions. In season two, for example, Bauer compelled terrorist Syed Ali to cooperate by staging a mock execution of Ali's family, but stopped short of actually killing them. Bauer's refusal to cross that line, to kill innocents—especially females and children—marked the essential moral difference between Bauer and Ali, and by extension between the civilized U.S. and our savage adversaries.

But by season three that restraint would seem quaint, as Bauer kidnapped Steven Saunders's daughter—both a female and a child—and was perfectly willing to infect her with a deadly virus if Saunders did not comply. Saving civilization required erasing the very defining border of civilization established in the previous season. Not only was Bauer willing to cross his own moral line, the narrative dictated that crossing it was the only thing that could save millions of lives— and thus the audience was supposed to be willing to cross that line as well.

That willingness is the measure of Bauer's worth. Whether the enemy is foreign invaders, domestic terrorists, or gutless bureaucrats, Bauer is distinguished by his willingness and ability, whatever the cost, to go as far as he must—decapitations or mutilations, torture or treason, fratricide or patricide—to rise to the challenge of the enemy and match brutality with brutality. Damn the rules. Damn the consequences. In so doing, "Jack Bauer" has emerged in our War on Terrorism culture as a mythic hero whom Tom Tancredo knew would be readily understood as shorthand for the proposition that in the War on Terrorism the acceptable means are any means necessary.[7]

Conservatives have cheered 24's "get tough" attitude, and prominent Republican fans include Secretary Chertoff, Limbaugh, Supreme Court Judge Antonin Scalia, and "24 fanatic" President George H.W. Bush (Tapper). A friend of Surnow's describes the conservative writing staff as "like a Hollywood television annex to the White House. It's like an auxiliary wing" (Mayer). And it's easy to see why. Jack Bauer would no doubt share the Bush Administration's view that the Geneva Conventions are "quaint," support Bush's use of wiretaps without a warrant, and favor Bush's expansion of "extraordinary rendition"—the kidnapping of people and shipping them off to secret prisons in foreign countries to be tortured.

Yet despite the politics of the series and the outspokenness of its self-described "right wing nut job" co-creator Surnow, 24's appeal extends beyond conservatives. 24's producers cite Barbra Streisand and Bill Clinton as fans. I personally know progressive luminaries who watch the show. And I'm sure many in the 24 audience can sympathize with writer Sarah Vowell's feeling guilty for using the same credit card to donate to Amnesty International that she used to buy 24 DVDs.

While it may seem surprising that there are fans for whom watching 24 seems to require both a suspension of disbelief and a suspension of beliefs, 24's appeal across the political divide should not really come as a surprise. Skill, strength, and speed are attractive qualities, regardless of political persuasion. Quick-thinking, resourceful, decisive, and fearless, Jack Bauer is, if not a superhero, at least a heightened human. His instincts more acute, his reflexes more agile, his will more intense, his endurance stronger, Bauer allows us to partake vicariously of those strengths in measures most people do not usually experience.

Early in our war in Afghanistan, on an October 13, 2001 CNBC broadcast, *New York Times* columnist Thomas Friedman, a center-liberal with hawkish tendencies, explained that while he had been a critic of Defense

---

[7] 24 does recognize the value of abilities beyond the traditional martial virtues. Jack may be a loner, but he is not totally independent. He relies on Chloe, who is just as vital as he is to national security. Skill with a computer is depicted as equally important as skill with a gun. Even though the film aesthetics of the keyboard and the computer screen are nowhere near as developed as are the aesthetics of traditional symbols of power like the gun, the horse, or the car, the series solidifies the full-fledged emergence of the tech-wizard as a new kind of hero alongside the gunfighter, the street cop, and the special-ops ranger.

Secretary Donald Rumsfeld before the war, "there's one thing . . . that I do like about Rumsfeld. He is just a little bit crazy, and in this kind of war, [the terrorists] always count on being able to out-crazy us, and I'm glad we got some guy on our bench . . . who's just a little bit crazy, not totally, but you never know what that guy's going to do, and I say that's my guy."[8]

I suspect Friedman's view of Rumsfeld captures some of Bauer's appeal for liberal audiences: there is something exciting in the visceral, kinetic power of Bauer's focused recklessness, in his audaciousness, in his ability to go where we cannot and take us with him as he breaks through the restraints that contain the rest of us. Jack Bauer can do what you could never dream of. And get away with it. And that feels liberating. Kind of like a Chris Rock routine (but with violence) or the socially accepted narcissism of pop stars—it is (generally) unlikely that I would carry myself with Mick Jagger's swagger, but I do get a kick out of watching him strut and fret his hour upon the stage.

Furthermore, despite the politics of some of its writers, *24* does not blindly follow a conservative line or celebrate the Bush administration. The show's villains have included military hawks, greedy oil companies trying to use war to manipulate oil markets, and politicians willing to shred civil liberties and inter Muslims in detention camps. For a conservative show made during a conservative presidency there is a surprising frequency with which *24*'s America is betrayed by self-proclaimed patriots claiming to serve it.

Characters like National Security Advisor Roger Stanton and the Coral Snake soldiers in the second season, presidential aide Walt Cummings and President Charles Logan in the fifth season, and Jack's own father and brother in the sixth season are among the many who betray America—both its people and its principles—in the name of "patriotism." Those who claim to love America can be, in fact always have been, as dangerous as those who claim to hate America.

These depictions of powerful figures engaging in antidemocratic and militaristic excesses dramatize the liberal critique of the Bush administration for its repeated violations of constitutional norms and limitations. Indeed, when confronted by President Palmer, Stanton justified his actions

---

[8] In time, "a little bit crazy" and a lot incompetent proved too much for Friedman, however, and he eventually joined the chorus of people calling for Rumsfeld's ouster. It seems "a little bit crazy" just might work better on TV than in real life.

by parroting the Republican charge that the Democrats' defense policy is too passive and insisted that he was trying to give the Palmer presidency "some balls" (2-13). Sentiments of which our own Vice President Dick "we must work the dark side" Cheney, a 24 fan, would probably approve.

There might be something more to explain the liberal attraction to 24 and the way it functions as wish fulfillment even for those who don't share its surface politics. There is an implicit critique—perhaps even a yearning—throughout 24. 24 is not just a fantasy after all, but a *compensatory* fantasy: Bauer and CTU win the battles that Bush and the Republicans have not. Bush's real world incompetence makes necessary Bauer's fantasy world omnipotence. 24 is both counter and companion to Aaron Sorkin's left-leaning *The West Wing*. If *The West Wing* offered the fantasy of the Clinton Administration without Monica Lewinsky, 24 offers the fantasy of the Bush Administration without, well, the Bush Administration.

Ask yourself, what would Jack Bauer have done if he, rather than President Bush, had received the intelligence report entitled "Bin Laden Determined to Attack in the United States" just weeks before September 11? Had Bauer been running the FBI rather than Robert Mueller, can you imagine the Bureau failing to follow up on the concerns of Colleen Rowley and other FBI field agents about Zacarias Moussaoui's training to fly airliners without learning to take off or land? Given faulty evidence to justify the U.S. launching a unilateral war in the Mideast CIA director George Tenet declared it was "a slam dunk," Jack Bauer discovered it was a forgery.[9] What if Bauer had been in charge of Walter Reed hospital? Or the Iraqi Coalition Provisional Authority? If Jack Bauer had been doing a "heck of a job" running FEMA, instead of Michael Brown, how long would it have taken to evacuate New Orleans? *Before* Hurricane Katrina hit. Something tells me, oh, twenty-four hours. About as long it would have taken Bauer to get Osama bin Laden. Dead or alive. Year after year, threat after threat, Jack Bauer fulfills our frustrated desire for a government equal to the challenges of the day.[10]

Not everyone is going along with the ride, of course. *Newsweek* has suggested that the show may be a "neocon sex fantasy" and Sidney

---

[9] This point was suggested by James Poniewozik's "The Evolution of Jack Bauer."

[10] Perhaps Surnow and Sorkin should collaborate with Martin Sheen and Keifer Sutherland on a *West Wing/24* crossover show, giving the audience a combination of Josiah Bartlett's ethics and Jack Bauer's effectiveness.

Blumenthal was even more blunt, labeling the series "torture porn" (Gordon, Blumenthal). The Parents Television Council has noted that from 2002–2005, *24* led a sixfold increase over the previous four years in prime-time TV torture. Of special concern was the rise in the number of *protagonists* using torture (Gorman).

Some in the creative community have also responded. As a corrective to *24*'s excesses, other TV series like *Without a Trace* and *The Unit* have tried to show torture more realistically. Shawn Ryan, an executive producer on *The Unit*, explained "we tried to show the futility of [torture] and how it hurts both parties" adding "how much useful information was pulled from Abu Ghraib, probably none. But how much damage did it do to America around the world?" (Miller). Perhaps the most succinct criticism came from David Danzig, director of the Prime Time Torture Project of Human Rights First, who simply observed "it's unthinkable that Captain Kirk would torture someone" (Miller).

In its sixth season *24* seemed both to flout those criticisms, by having Bauer cut the finger off a Russian diplomat for instance, and accommodate them by acknowledging thorough the characterization of Jack's brother Graem and father Phillip the ease with which Bauer's "do whatever you decide is necessary" attitude can slide into a sociopathic self-righteousness. When Graem confessed, under Jack's torture, to ordering the assassination of David Palmer, Tony Almeida, Michelle Dessler, and Jack himself, and justified it by telling a horrified Jack, "I love my country and in the real world sometimes that means you have to do things, terrible things, even unforgivable things, for the sake of your country" (6-7), it was easy to imagine the same words coming out of Jack's mouth and hard to miss the family resemblance—indeed, this statement is practically the Bauer family motto. When a defiant Graem insisted that he and Jack were "the same," the depth of Jack's rage could not silence—in fact, it rather enhanced—the ring of truth in Graem's accusation. This is a truth that Jack cannot kill. These Bauer boys understand each other very well.

The producers here seem to acknowledge that there is something vaguely aristocratic, certainly antidemocratic, and truly threatening in this shadowy dynasty of white, privileged men empowered to disregard what is legal or moral in pursuit of their own version of what is necessary. Watching Jack, Graem, and papa Phillip (also part of the season six conspiracy), one wonders just what terrible things, even unforgivable things, these people would *not* do once they convinced themselves that they were for the sake of "their" country.

Phillip and Graem's treachery occurred in the midst of 24's pervasive atmosphere of betrayal and uncertainty, an atmosphere linked to our real-world sense of anxiety and isolation in a post–Cold War, post-9/11 world of unstable alliances and unpredictable threats. And this is where 24's ideology regarding violence becomes especially important. 24's unflinching depiction of torture and violence does not really glamorize violence, it sanctifies it. In 24's version of our world, words may be hollow, allegiances may shift, your closest intimates may deceive and betray, but *violence clarifies*. In a world of deception and betrayal, force allows you to dispel ambiguity. Force allows you to get to the heart of things. Force allows you to discern the truth. And in 24's world, where threats typically cannot be outwitted, cannot be contained and must, ultimately, be killed, force empowers Bauer, and through him us, to reimpose order on a chaotic and threatening universe.

24 executive producer/writer Howard Gordon has defended Bauer's use of torture by pointing out the toll that his actions have taken on him: "Jack is basically damned," he told Mayer. And no doubt Bauer has lost a lot in the service of his country: his wife was killed by his ex-mistress; his daughter abandoned him; his girlfriend left him; his president, his mentor, his brother, and his father all tried to kill him. Love, blood, nationality, even paternity are unreliable—no ties truly bind.[11] Having been turned on by colleagues and siblings, lovers and mentors, parents and presidents, an increasing sense of isolation and desperation seems to underlie Bauer's actions.

But rendering Bauer's dilemma as strictly individual misses the point. It is not just personal psyche but national honor that is implicated. Bauer's most brazen violations of policy—breaking Hector Salazar out of prison, torturing prisoners, raiding foreign embassies—typically have

---

[11] Father-son enmity has become something of a 24 obsession—the last three seasons have featured fathers or father figures trying to kill their sons: Navi tried to kill Berooz in season four, Chris Henderson tried to kill Jack in season five, and Philip Bauer killed Graem and tried to kill Jack in season six, the same season in which Jack not only allowed his father to be killed but also threatened to kill his father figure/potential father-in-law James Heller.

the backing of the (usually black, and thus presumably liberal) president and of the viewer. Bauer is no loose cannon. He is a cannon aimed by those in command and cheered by those in the audience. And while Bauer may pay a price for his actions, *America* does not.

24's producers do not—perhaps can not—acknowledge that Bauer's damnation would not be his alone, that his damnation would be replicated on a nationwide and international scale. Exploiting the anxieties and issues of our time but not truly engaging them, 24 fails to assess the price—ethical, political, and yes, spiritual—of fighting the War on Terrorism Bauer's way. What would the price of Jack's raid on the Chinese embassy be when measured in heightened tensions with China? How would Russia react to Jack's dismemberment of their consul general at the Russian embassy? Would the fallout of a president illegally detaining journalists or ordering innocent Americans into concentration camps be disgust for the president or disdain for the constitution?

No matter Bauer's personal pain, in 24 the *nation* never has wounds to heal, or crimes to cleanse. Bauer has instead taken on our suffering—died, spiritually, for our sins (he even physically died and was resurrected in season two). It is a tactical fantasy that the nation can stay safely immune from whatever "solely" personal price Jack must pay. A fantasy that leaves the audience off the hook, comfortably enjoying the fruits of Bauer's violence without ever having been asked by the show to interrogate our own desires—much less take responsibility for them.

Instead, deniability is standard operating procedure. Covert missions, off-book tactics, Bauer resigning so he can torture as a "private citizen"—all are designed to elide responsibility and evade accountability. And lack of responsibility and accountability—the contempt of congressional subpoenas; the undermining of checks and balances; the suffocating of debate by restricting information; the misleading at best, perjurious at worst, testimony of administration officials and Supreme Court nominees—are perhaps the defining characteristics of our political moment. That aversion to accountability, combined with the faith in the saving power of force, perhaps more than anything else make 24 truly a show of our time.

Some might counsel not to take 24 too seriously—that, as Rush Limbaugh says, "it's just a television show" (Mayer). But it is hard to give credence to views like that in light of the emotional power that a show like

24 can wield on its audiences and when, as Jim Carafano shrewdly observed at the Heritage Foundation symposium, people "invest 24 hours of their life watching 24" but don't "spend 24 hours of their life seriously really thinking and reading and studying" the issues in the show. (Sorry, Rush, it is disingenuous to hail the series for its pro-American values and then claim that the series' values are unimportant). And such protestations are not comforting when we remember that people at the highest echelons of power are watching—and celebrating—24 and may very well agree with Surnow's assertion that "America wants the War on Terror fought by Jack Bauer" and with commentator Laura Ingraham's rather breathtaking claim that 24's popularity is tantamount to a national referendum approving torture (Mayer).

Some may object more generally that our popular culture has always expressed, even been a necessary escape valve for, our ambivalence about and impatience with democracy and due process. But let's not pretend that our antidemocratic inclinations have been neatly channeled into a hermetically sealed popular culture, there safely contained, the domain solely of cowboys, gangsters, and caped (or hooded) crusaders. No, indeed. The borders between fantasy and reality are porous and those antidemocratic impulses have overflown the pages of our pulp novels and matinee movie screens. They raged through our lynch mobs and internment camps, witch hunts and jury boxes, massacres and mass incarcerations. Leo Frank learned something about them. So did Emmett Till. And our brothers and sisters at Wounded Knee. And at My Lai. As did Rodney King. And James Byrd.

So whenever I am tempted to conclude that 24 is just harmless fun rather than a guilty pleasure, I confront again the words of cultural historian Richard Slotkin eloquently reminding us that

> [t]he primary social and political function of the *extraordinary* violence of myth is to sanction the ordinary violence of oppression, and injustice, of brutalities casual or systematic, of the segregation, insult or humiliation of targeted groups. . . . [W]hen the nation faces a challenge from beyond its borders, the mythology of vigilantism reminds us that extraordinary violence by privileged heroes, often acting in despite of law, has been the means of our national salvation. (Slotkin 192–193, emphasis in original)

And I wonder if the public's disturbingly high level of tolerance for torture and our leaders' contempt for due process and disdain for the constitution—the very instrument designed to embody and call us to account for our deepest values—are aided and abetted by the success of popular entertainments that argue that such tragedies are necessities.

In what is surely the best piece of writing about 24 in the popular press, Jane Mayer recounts the November 2006 meeting of some of 24's creative team with military and human rights experts to discuss the show's depiction of torture. A key participant was the dean of the U.S. Military Academy at West Point, General Patrick Finnegan. Mayer reports Finnegan explaining that

> . . . it had become increasingly hard to convince some cadets that America had to respect the rule of law and human rights, even when terrorists did not. One reason for the growing resistance he suggested was misperceptions spread by 24 which was exceptionally popular with his students. As he told me, "The kids see it, and say 'if torture is wrong what about 24?'"

This kind of critique from high-ranking military officers, precisely the ones one might assume would approve of 24's message that the U.S. should take off the gloves, might seem counterintuitive. But to their credit, and our relief, these are the very people who understand that the popularization of Bauer's methods poses a threat both to America's international standing and to America's soldiers should they be captured.

In fact, it is instructive to look at the evolution of our methods of "enhanced interrogation." While the term itself owes its beginnings to, yes, Hitler's Gestapo (Sullivan), the techniques that we have been using were based in part on what we thought the Soviets and the Chinese would do if they captured American soldiers (Shane). Thus our fears, our fantasies, about the worst in our enemies became the blueprint for the worst in ourselves.

Why shouldn't we expect this process of projection to be reversed? Why shouldn't we expect that our contemporary enemies, with absolutely no reason to believe that Jack Bauer and Abu Ghraib are not the American norm, would model their behavior on these examples?

What might they do to us if their image of what we do to them is shaped by what Howard Gordon calls 24's "improvisations in sadism" (Mayer)? Might we be providing our adversaries with fantasies that, filtered through their fear and rage, will become the blueprint for tragedy for our own soldiers? If this concern seems more fanciful than practical, consider the assertion of Jack Cloonan, a former secret service agent with the FBI's bin Laden squad in New York, that trainees in former al-Qaeda camps watched movie videos "to get ideas" (Donaldson James).

Joel Surnow ignores these kinds of concerns, blithely telling Mayer, "It's not like somebody goes, 'Oh look what they're doing, I'll do that.' Is it?" Well, apparently, yes. Tony Lagouranis told Reuters that in Iraq U.S. soldiers "got an open ended interrogation rule . . . saying you can basically do whatever the hell you want," and explained that "in the absence of training, because we weren't trained how to torture, we turned to what we saw on television" (Gorman). "People watch the shows and then walk into the interrogation booths and do the same things they've just seen," he explained to Mayer.

Just as on the homefront we worry about television's impact on children when used as an "electronic babysitter," on the battlefront television seems to have become an electronic military instructor. "That's all people did in Iraq was watch DVDs of television shows and movies. What we learned in military schools didn't apply anymore," Lagouranis told the LA Times, adding that, "everyone wanted to be a Hollywood interrogator" (Miller).

Our fantasies can become truly dangerous when we mistake them for realities. Americans have historically paid—and exacted—a terrible price for past attempts to play Hollywood heroes. After the Vietnam War, veterans and medical professionals identified a complex mix of stress, self-hatred, and feeling of failure experienced by soldiers unable to live up to the stoic heroism projected in the fantasies of their day. This became known as John Wayne Syndrome:

> [The] internalization of an ideal of superhuman military bravery, skill, and invulnerability to guilt and grief, which is identified at some point with "John Wayne". . . as a figure of speech, signifying the supposed perfection of soldierly masculinity. Since that ideal is, in fact, impossible to live up to,

"John Wayne Syndrome" often took the form of excessive guilt or shame for feelings of guilt or grief, or for responding to battlefield stress with a normal human mix of fear and bravery. Disillusion with the Wayne ideal, or recognition of its inapplicability in the real world of combat, could transform the heroic symbol into its opposite, a metaphor of false consciousness, pretension, and military excess. (Slotkin 519–520)

In fact, "false consciousness, pretension, and military excess," a desire to play out a John Wayne script on the stage of Southeast Asia, could well stand as a description of America's Vietnam War policy. By imaging ourselves as John Wayne, clinging to the fantasy as a reliable guide to reality, John Wayne Syndrome, then, becomes more than a description of personal failure. It becomes a prescription for policy failure, a summation of how we went into a war that went so wrong.

Forty years later we are in danger of creating a Jack Bauer Syndrome—both a desire to imitate Bauer's efficient brutality and the inevitable letdown when Bauer's tactics don't produce the expected real-world results. What happens when a nineteen-year-old soldier who inculcates and emulates the Bauer posture meets defiance from a prisoner or restrictions from a superior officer? Does he defy protocol and pull a "Jack Bauer"? Does he shoot a prisoner? Assault a fellow officer? Ignore a presidential order?

What happens when that young soldier finds that the methods of Bauer's madness do not produce the same results in real life—do not give him instant information or the power to take down a terrorist cell? Does that frustrated soldier retreat into a shadow of shame, inadequacy, and self-hatred for not being tough enough, not being "Jack Bauer" enough? Or does he lash out even harder, convinced that more force, more aggression, more willingness to disregard the Geneva conventions, or the U.S. Constitution, are what is necessary?

As with the John Wayne Syndrome, Jack Bauer Syndrome has policy, as well as psychological, implications. The invasion of Iraq was our national Jack Bauer moment. It exhibited the same reckless commitment to unilateral action, the same impatience with procedure and due process, the same sense of entitlement to use extraordinary violence, the same willingness and ability to go as far we wanted: Damn the rules. Damn the consequences.

The belief that we'd be greeted with flowers and chocolates by the people of Iraq, that we could use those people as blank slates on which we could write our own version of a Western-style, American-friendly democracy in the heart of the Arab world, that breaking Saddam would send shock waves of democratization throughout the region, that in wartime the president is a law unto himself, accountable to no one but himself, these—and the tragic, painful consequences, for us and for them—all bear witness to our national Jack Bauer Syndrome: a disregard for standards of restraint and cooperation; an unrealistic belief in the power of force to clarify, establish dominance, quell chaos, and assert control. But as in Vietnam, political reality, somehow, stubbornly, failed to follow our political fantasy.

For almost the length of the War on Terrorism, Surnow and 24 have given us Jack Bauer as an idealized image of how the United States of America must fight that war: ruthlessly, unrelentingly, dispassionately. Since 24's premiere just weeks after September 11, 2001, Bauer, like many Americans, has bought the neocon notion that it is better to be feared than loved. But by the conclusion of season six, Bauer, like many Americans, appeared to have the beginnings of buyer's remorse.

At the end of that season, with America's trust in its president at a nadir and the world's trust in America strained if not shattered, 24 gave us the image of Jack Bauer at "a crossroads" (6-24): abandoned, embittered, shunned, and betrayed. It was in this moment that 24 emerged as a twenty-first-century version of John Ford's seminal Western *The Searchers* and Jack Bauer took his place as the Ethan Edwards of our time.

The Searchers presented the American hero as paradox: Edwards's relentless drive, his intimate knowledge of the enemy, and his skill in warfare make him indispensable for the survival of the embattled White settler community, but his disdain for authority, his poisonous race hatred, and almost uncontrollable violence mean that he can never truly be part of that community. In the iconic final image of the door closing on John Wayne as Edwards, excluding him from hearth and home, he— and perhaps more importantly we—understand that the very things that make Edwards fit to protect society make him unfit to live in it. Like a guard dog whose viciousness makes him both indispensable to the household and ineligible to enter it, Edwards's fate is to remain the eternal sentry: vigilant, watchful, essential. But outside. Forever outside.

A half century after *The Searchers*, John Wayne's frontier hero has become Kiefer Sutherland's counterterrorist operative. The buttes of Monument Valley have become the skyscrapers of Los Angeles. The "Indians" have become terrorists. At the conclusion of season six Jack, like Ethan Edwards, had a homecoming that emphasized his inability to come home. Told by James Heller to stay away from his daughter Audrey, that Bauer was cursed to bring ruin to those he touched, that he was unable to stay out of "the game" and that Audrey would pay the price just as Bauer's wife did, Bauer retreated from the home of Secretary Heller, the father who rejected him. As alone as Edwards, with gun in hand and intimations of suicidal desperation, he stood on a cliff, literally at the edge of the abyss, at the periphery of the country which he had served and from which he had been severed, and stared at the waves of the Pacific Ocean, with no frontier left and nowhere left to go.

Like Edwards, through bitter quests and bloody deeds, Bauer has become so consumed by his mission, so transformed by its cruel necessities, so tainted by what he must become—the darkness he must indulge—to protect home and homeland that he can now find no place within them. His saving, even messianic, power separates him, makes him necessary and necessarily different, places him forever outside the society he serves. Bauer can make love or he can make war but he cannot make both. This is his choice. This is the price that the hero must pay in the mythology of our nation.

This may have its appeal as an elegiac trope or poetic pose, but if we actually buy this mythology, what does it mean for our real soldiers on the frontlines abroad or our police on the streets of our cities? Must they too be "damned" by what their country has sent them to do and "cursed" by the consequences? Do we accept that losing one's family must be the price for protecting it? Is that the sacrifice we demand of our brothers and sisters? And if we demand this of them will we in time, like Heller, reject them as damaged goods?

Or, alternately, if Surnow is right that we want the War on Terrorism fought by Jack Bauer, what if our men and women in uniform are not as damaged, not as scarred, as Bauer? Are we then to conclude that they were unwilling to do terrible things, even unforgivable things, for the sake of their country? Were they therefore insufficiently tough, insufficiently patriotic? Do we then reject them as not army strong enough, not all that they could be?

Exactly what do we say to Tony Lagouranis, who suffered from panic attacks and "completely broke down" upon his return, when he—and all those like him—says to us—to each and every one of us—"I'm from New York City. I'm college-educated. But you put me in Iraq and told me to torture, and I did it, and I regretted it later" (McKelvey)?

Jack Bauer insisted on a similar reckoning in the finale of season six. In a scene we must pray is merely poignant, not prescient, Bauer held a gun on the former secretary of defense, his former boss, his betrayer, and protested, in a voice burning with hurt and bitterness, "The only thing I did, the only thing I have ever done, is what you and people like you have asked of me." How many returning veterans will soon be saying *that* to their country? As well they should. For how different, really, is carelessly sending a soldier into combat without body armor, sufficient troop levels, or credible war and post-war planning, from abandoning him in a Chinese prison?

Throughout the series Bauer has resembled Avner, the tormented leader of an antiterrorist assassination squad in Steven Spielberg's *Munich*, of whom a colleague says, "You do any terrifying thing you're asked to do, but you have to do it running. You think you can outrun your fears, your doubts. The only thing that really scares you . . . is stillness." Bauer, too, does it all running. When you run, your doubts and your demons may trail safely behind you, but in that stillness, when you stop, as Bauer did at key moments in season six, those doubts and demons have a chance to catch up. It was those moments when Bauer failed, or when the price of his successes became apparent, that season six was most compelling.

For all the intensity, adrenaline. and testosterone of 24 it was in the helpless torment seared onto Sutherland's face as Bauer watched the nuclear blast in Valencia, in Bauer's uncomprehending hurt and frothy rage at the revelation of Graem's betrayal, and in Bauer's embittered bewilderment during the closing moments of the season finale, that Jack Bauer was, perhaps, most alive as a character. That torment, that hurt, that rage, that bewilderment—and the fearlessness with which

Sutherland committed to them—made Bauer, in those moments, seem more real than he ever had.

Perhaps this version of Jack Bauer seemed so real also because he seemed so recognizable. Artists old enough to remember the aftermath of the Vietnam War, and a good deal more honest that our politicians, have begun reminding us that the price of our fight is a question due to become more and more pressing because soon, very soon, a very expensive bill will arrive.

And so we are seeing this version of Jack Bauer in other places: We have seen this version of Jack Bauer in the hero of Spielberg's 2005 *War of the Worlds* (which along with *The Terminal* and *Munich* can best be understood as comprising Spielberg's stunning 9/11 trilogy [or adding *Minority Report*, his 9/11 tetralogy]), who as Armond White has pointed out is also a modern Ethan Edwards: the blood on his hands, the reality of what he had to do to protect his family, keeping him, ultimately, outside of it.

We have heard this version of Jack Bauer in the haunted soldier-singer of Bruce Springsteen's "Devils & Dust," who sings, "I've got my finger on the trigger. And tonight faith just ain't enough. When I look into my heart, there's just devils and dust. I got God on my side. And I'm just trying to survive. What if what you do to survive kills the things you love? Fear's a powerful thing. It can turn your heart black you can trust. It'll take your God-filled soul and fill it with devils and dust."

We have seen this version of Jack Bauer in his, frankly, more-layered kindred spirit Kara "Starbuck" Thrace on *Battlestar Galactica*, ordered in the show's second season to assassinate her commander's rival, every muscle in her body fighting against her orders, against the horrifying idea that necessity has trumped morality and that she has now, and perhaps quite literally, become her enemy.

And, most urgently, we are seeing this version of Jack Bauer among us as Tony Lagouranis confesses, "I didn't know I would discover and indulge in my own evil" and "now that it has surfaced, I fear that it will be my constant companion for the rest of my life."[12]

Make no mistake: Bauer's crossroads is *our* crossroads, his dilemma *our* dilemma. If Jack Bauer is "damned," so are we. Each and every one

---

[12] Excerpt from Lagouranis's book, cowritten with Allen Mikaelian, *Fear Up Harsh: An Army Interrogator's Dark Journey Through Iraq*, cited in Tara McKelvey's "Torturer's Toll."

of us. If fighting the War on Terrorism requires creating a nation of Ethan Edwardses and Jack Bauers too damaged, too broken, too haunted to be accepted in the American family, what does this portend for America's position in the family of nations? As we violate treaties and alienate allies, must America, like Bauer, be shunned as too dangerous, too violent, too willing to break the rules in order to pursue our own vision? Must America, like Bauer, be viewed as cursed, bringing ruin to those who would get close to us? Must Bauer's fate, the fate of Cain, to be "a fugitive and a wanderer on the Earth," be the U.S.'s fate as well?

The myths we tell ourselves, how we imagine ourselves, matter, because in time what we imagine may become what we strive to be. Not surprisingly, if we continue to imagine ourselves as Jack Bauer, we may very well become Jack Bauer: isolated, scarred, bringing pain to those who love us and spurned by those we would love.

ERIC GREENE is a graduate of Stanford Law School and Wesleyan University. Greene is a civil rights activist in Los Angeles where his professional hats have also included writer, actor, and commentator on politics and the arts. Greene's first book was the critically acclaimed *Planet of the Apes as American Myth: Race, Politics and Popular Culture*. Hailed as "groundbreaking," the book has been reissued in numerous editions, including a Japanese translation. He is also, proudly, a returning contributor to BenBella Books having examined *Star Trek* and Cold War politics in BenBella's *Boarding the Enterprise*, *Battlestar Galactica*'s treatment of 9-11/Iraq War anxieties in *So Say We All*, and the role of faith in the Wheedonverse in *Serenity Found*.

REFERENCES

Blumenthal, Sidney. "From Norman Rockwell to Abu Ghraib." *Salon.com.* April 26, 2007.

Donaldson James, Susan. "Nuclear Blast on TV's '24' Causes Fallout for Fox." abcnews.com. January 15, 2007.

Gordon, Devin. "Die Another Day." *Newsweek.* January 12, 2007.

Gorman, Steve. "TV Torture Scenes Trouble Human Rights Activists." *Reuters.* March 8, 2007.

Kahn, Joseph. "China Executes Former Food and Drug Regulator." *New York Times.* July 11, 2007.

Lithwick. Dahlia. "Invisible Men," *Slate.com*, February 16, 2006.

Mayer, Jane. "Whatever It Takes." *The New Yorker.* February 19, 2007.

McCain, Senator John. "Torture's Terrible Toll," *Newsweek.* November 21, 2005.

McKelvey, Tara. "Torturer's Toll." *The American Prospect Online.* March 26, 2007.

Miller, Martin. "'24' Gets a Lesson in Torture from the Experts." *Los Angeles Times*, February 13, 2007.

Poniewozik, James. "The Evolution of Jack Bauer." *Time.* January 14, 2007.

Shane, Scott, and Mark Mazzetti. "Advisers Fault Harsh Methods in Interrogation." *Herald Tribune*, 30 May 2007.

Slotkin, Richard. *Gunfighter Nation.* New York: Atheneum, 1992.

Sullivan, Andrew. "Verschärfte Vernehmung." *Atlantic.com.* May 29, 2007.

Tapper, Jake. "Conservative Lovefest for '24.'" abcnews.go.com. June 23, 2006.

Taylor, Stuart. "How Not to Make Terrorism Policy." *The Atlantic Online.* June 5, 2007.

White, Armond. "Refugees and Searchers Go to the Movies." First of the Month.com, December, 2005.